XENOPHON
THE ATHENIAN

XENOPHON
THE ATHENIAN

The Problem of the Individual
and the Society of the *Polis*

By W. E. Higgins

State University of New York Press
Albany, 1977

Published by
State University of New York Press, Albany

© 1977 State University of New York

All rights reserved

Grateful acknowledgment is made to Random House, Inc. for permission to reprint material from "September 1, 1939," by W. H. Auden, from *The Collected Poetry of W. H. Auden*. Copyright 1940 by W. H. Auden.

Printed in the United States of America

No part of this book may be used or reproduced in any manner whatsoever without written permission. No part of this book may be stored in a retrieval system or transmitted in any form or by any means including electronic, electrostatic, magnetic tape, mechanical, photocopying, recording, or otherwise without the prior permission in writing of the publisher.

For information, contact State University of New York Press, Albany, NY
www.sunypress.edu

Library of Congress Cataloging-in-Publication Data
Higgins, William Edward, 1945-
    Xenophon the Athenian.
    Includes bibliographical references.
    ISBN 978-0-87395-369-6 (hardcover : alk. paper)
    ISBN 978-0-7914-7652-9 (pbk. : alk. paper)
    1. Xenophon—Criticism and interpretation.
1. Title

PA4497.H5　　　　　　　　　1977　　　　　　　　938'.007'2024 [B]

77-2392

To the memory of my father

CONTENTS

Preface xi

Chapter 1   READING XENOPHON 1

Chapter 2   SOCRATES 21

Chapter 3   CYRUS 44

Chapter 4   TYRANNY 60

Chapter 5   THE ACTIVE LIFE 76

Chapter 6   HISTORY 99

Chapter 7   XENOPHON AND ATHENS 128

Abbreviations 144

Notes... 145

Index... 180

PREFACE

A new book on Xenophon hardly requires apology, but a few words may be in order about the aims and methods of the present volume. It is, above all, a book about Xenophon qua Xenophon and makes no attempt to satisfy the interests of those who read Xenophon for information about military tactics, fourth-century economics, history, and so forth. It confronts the text of Xenophon as that text exists in itself and proceeds on the assumption that the text must be understood on its own terms and within its own limits, especially since there is no good reason for believing that any work of Xenophon exists in a form today other than that which he himself desired. The book, in short, asks the question "what is here" rather than the question "what ought to be here." Its argument also progresses through a close reading of the text which may often seem at first glance a mere rewording of Xenophon's original but which ought to prove something more salient upon closer inspection. By the same token, highlights in the discussion of one work ought to be borne in mind when similar topics appear in the exposition of another. The reader is invited to make his own connections, for they are often not spelled out.

The book's basic attitude will also be evident in the notes, where the majority of references are to the texts of Xenophon and not to the works of scholars. I have generally confined citations of such secondary materials to places where different views are maintained or where surveys of problems can conveniently be found. I have not attempted, moreover, to list every opinion on every point or to counter by name and in detail all those who argue for views contrary to those taken here. To have done so would have increased the size of the book inordinately and have inevitably led to a subtle misplacement of passion by putting a greater emphasis on the writings of scholars when primacy of attention should be accorded to those of Xenophon. Nevertheless I trust I have not failed to consider any important work on Xenophon which appeared before the summer of 1975.

Secondly, the book attempts to see all the works of Xenophon as forming one man's creative production, in the belief that comprehension of his total *oeuvre* and the relation of individual parts to one another may facilitate a better understanding of Xenophon's works when taken separately. Such an approach has not been common, and those who have attempted it have often operated under what one reader feels to be false preconceptions, or they have been content to catalogue and cross reference Xenophon's ideas without actually interpreting them. I have singled out one controlling idea, Xenophon's understanding of the relation between the individual and the *polis*, because it is something which unifies all of Xenophon's varied literary endeavors and because it has not been treated with emphasis though many have recognized its importance. As the ensuing pages will demonstrate, however, the argument makes no claim that this is the only important idea in Xenophon or that it is the only one unifying his angles of outlook. Indeed it is impossible to treat so central a theme in an exclusive way, without directing attention to related issues (for example, the family, finance, interstate relations) and dealing with them as complementary to the key concern.

Naturally all Xenophon's works are examined, except the *Kynegetikos* whose authenticity is still doubted; but the order of their discussion, arranged to juxtapose complementary themes, implies nothing about beliefs concerning the order of their composition.

Finally, the book deliberately avoids dealing with tired and tiresome questions like the problem of the historical Socrates or the search for a detailed relationship between Xenophon's life and the chronology of his writing. On the latter point, especially, too many scholars have gone too far in their desire for certitude when the genuine evidence is so small. They have entrapped themselves in methodological circles; and, arguing from the supposed facts of Xenophon's life obtained from his works, they try to establish the times these works were composed and to use material so derived to explain Xenophon's ideas. The biographical and intentional fallacies, in other words, have wrought interpretive havoc and have made one monumental essay in this area a monument of error. At the risk of proclaiming a self-fulfilling prophecy for the present undertaking, it is still worthwhile to repeat the remark of Field. "Few scholars," he said, "show at their best in dealing with Xenophon. There seems to be something about him which makes even the wisest of them lose all sense of the evidence."

There is one scholar, however, to whom this study owes an enormous debt. Leo Strauss has performed two great services for the understanding of Xenophon. He has displayed before the text a critical humility which should always have been present but which a scholarly tradition, more concerned to berate than explicate, seems to have lost. In the face of such hostile and belittling opinion, the respect and enthusiasm of such a keen mind for Xenophon's thought have been for a younger reader sharing this attitude a constant encouragement. But more important still, Strauss has understood, as few have, the absolute need when studying Xenophon to read between the lines and to appreciate the centrality of irony in a Socratic context. The Romantic and post-Romantic nineteenth-century scholarly traditions (Kierkegaard is an important exception) seem not to have appreciated what Mann has called "incomparably the most profound and alluring problem in the world," and one distinguished philologue writing in the present century has even dismissed irony as a critical magic wand, as the last expedient of despairing commentators.

It should be said, however, that the present work brings to bear upon Xenophon's text the intuitions of a student of literature rather than those of a political scientist. The writer on Xenophon must have a certain versatility, and I hope that concerns other than those of *belles-lettres* have not received short shrift.

If anything this work aims to reform some notions held about Xenophon, or, failing that, at least to invite readers to reexamine on their own old and received opinions, something a recent little book on Xenophon in the Classical Life and Letters series regretably fails to do. Those who wish may therefore see in the epithet attached to Xenophon in the title the mark of a quiet revisionism.

Doubtless more remains to be said; and there is always a feeling of inadequacy when confronted with a major author, a sense that he possesses a wisdom never fully apprehensible by most and certainly not by the young. Yet this book is offered in the confidence that its approach is a correct and much-needed one, even if some of its conclusions will be found unsatisfactory. Perhaps it will be good to recall the words the composer of *Pelléas* addressed to the composer of the *Firebird*. When Stravinsky asked him what he thought of the ballet, Debussy replied, "Que voulez-vous, il fallait bien commencer par quelque chose."

* * *

It is always a pleasure to acknowledge the help given by those whose expertise has insured for this book whatever value it possesses, and it especially befits a work on Xenophon, who so appreciated the importance of friends.

I first began my study of fourth-century Greece with Glen Bowersock, and he directed the dissertation of which the present undertaking is a thorough revision and elaboration. He has also been unstinting in his reading and criticizing of successive drafts, by which he has enabled me in his singular way to benefit from his own, sometimes different, points of view, without stifling my own sense of what I thought had to be said.

John Finley also read several drafts of this work from its earliest stage on, and he made suggestions on form and content which have made it better than it otherwise would have been. His ever lively and broad appreciation of Greek literature, coupled as it is with an imperial command of the Greek language, will always be an inspiration.

Perhaps only those who have similarly benefited will appreciate the extent of my indebtedness to Christopher Jones's meticulous reading of the manuscript and his humane devil's advocacy. Martin Ostwald also provided me with his own close reading which saved me from many slips, and he lent needed encouragement at a critical time. Two anonymous readers from the Press made well-taken comments and suggestions, which I have tried to follow.

To all these I offer what can only be inadequate thanks. For the inadequacies of the ensuing chapters, I, too, am solely responsible.

W.E.H.

Brandeis University
August 1976

1
READING XENOPHON

Votre âme est un paysage choisi
Que vont charmant masques et bergamasques
Jouant du luth et dansant et quasi
Tristes sous leurs déguisements fantasques.
— Verlaine

The sympathetic reader of Xenophon soon learns to savor the mutability of fortune. He has any number of reasons for doing so; but not the least among them will be his wondering realization that it is now a truth, universally acknowledged, that a simple author like Xenophon, who never managed to research his facts as well as he might have, cannot be taken seriously. Xenophon may amuse and entertain but hardly educate and inspire. But then even he had honestly to confess that his own teacher Socrates once called him a fool.[1] So Niebuhr had good authority to do likewise (though he seems not to have known it) when, in the first decades of the nineteenth century, he launched an attack from which Xenophon's reputation amongst the learned has yet to recover.[2] Xenophon is an author they condescend to, a squire in tweeds, tiresome and hardly rigorous. Yet how explain the interest of Machiavelli and the praise of Gibbon? For it appears that Machiavelli cites Xenophon more often than he does Plato and Aristotle,[3] while Gibbon calls him with succinct perspicacity "sage and heroic."[4] It is an irony Xenophon would have appreciated that the very simplicity of style which renders him so accessible to the beginner in Greek has charmed out of perception the scrutiny of scholars.

For, it has been observed, the danger in reading Xenophon is the feeling of fast comprehension which derives from the ease of his expression.[5] But where, or who, is Xenophon?

Philosopher, biographer, essayist, novelist, historian, he was a versatile talent and, let it be remembered, often a pioneering one. Yet his very versatility tends to hide him and to raise doubts. Can a novelist be a philosopher or aspire to writing history? Is it possible, or even worthwhile, to put together the guises of this Protean figure? The diversity of Xenophon intrigues, inviting study, perhaps a reassessment.

Socrates had a principle that one kind of investigation should begin with an examination of the most basic elements in a given problem.[6] A study of the Socratic Xenophon will thus fittingly commence with an examination of just such a fundamental feature, namely, the words and style in which he expressed himself. It may be that some of the present confusion about him stems from an initial failure to read him properly. Perhaps if how he writes is understood, what he writes may become evident more simply.

Lucid and graceful, Xenophon's style tries, as a rule, not to call attention to itself. It is quite often content with ordinary words and frequently enjoys the description of ordinary, even humdrum, things in a generally uncomplicated syntax. Thus Xenophon can write how two men from the ranks once interrupted him at breakfast with the discovery of a way across the Kentrites river:

> καὶ τότε ἔλεγον ὅτι τυγχάνοιεν φρύγανα συλλέγοντες ὡς ἐπὶ πῦρ, κἄπειτα κατίδοιεν ἐν τῷ πέραν ἐν πέτραις καθηκούσαις ἐπ' αὐτὸν τὸν ποταμὸν γέροντά τε καὶ γυναῖκα καὶ παιδίσκας ὥσπερ μαρσίπους ἱματίων κατατιθεμένους ἐν πέτρᾳ ἀντρώδει.
>
> And then they said that they happened to be collecting faggots for a fire and then looked down on an old man, his wife, and daughters on the other side, amongst the rocks which go down to the river itself, placing what seemed to be pouches of clothes in a hollowed rock.[7]

This by no means untypical passage has a directness about it which derives, at least in part, from its careful use of straightforward, concrete words like "faggots," "pouches," "rocks," and "clothes." The description contains what might be called the literary equivalent of a painting's tactile value as well as a quality of specificity; the men have not just been gathering wood, but wood for a fire, they saw not just a group but a definite family, and they looked not vaguely to the river's far side but to the point where rocks fell to the water. Xenophon makes no attempt to intrude himself; he lets the details speak for themselves, without flamboyance, making them all the more memorable, by keeping only what is needed. Sturdy and self-effacing, Xenophon achieves an elegance which is not effete.

He has, above all, a keen feeling for the precise possibilities of words. In his description of the Armenians' strange drinking habits he says, for example, that whenever anyone liked someone and wanted to toast him, he dragged him off to the wine krater, bent over, and drank up, "slurping *(rhophounta)*[8] like an ox." Xenophon does not use a neutral word like "drinking" but a more pungent and hardly genteel one which adds the right force and color to this scene depicting something raucous and slightly ridiculous. Without it the effect would have been bland and the character of the situation uncommunicated. But Xenophon can also describe equally well—and with becoming graciousness—how Greeks spoke and acted when drinking *chez* Kallias. There Kharmides has a mind still sufficiently unbefuddled to say that Socrates, in warning against the dangers of love, is trying to "spook" *(mormoluttei)*[9] his friends away from the handsome people; he does not simply turn them away or dissuade them. Kharmides has used not only an informal word suitable for an easy-going conversation but has also selected one which adds to the general hilarity with its comic suggestion that Socrates is trying to scare his companions as if he were an adult frightening a child with an unexpected "boo!" Thus Kharmides also implies that Socrates can certainly not expect to get away with what he is doing in so mature a company. Xenophon's ability to capitalize on a word so that it implies a theme as it describes a scene can also be seen when Socrates at the same symposium reports his success with Kritoboulos. He has just weaned Kritoboulos sufficiently away from Kleinias that he has even seen his young charge look at his formerly irresistible beloved and "blink" *(skardamuxanta)*.[10] He uses a common enough word to describe the youth's ever so slight return from seeming exaltation to ordinary reality, and at the same time he mirthfully puts in doubt the lastingness and scope of his alleged triumph. Finally, on a heroic level, Xenophon recounts how the Spartan king Agesilaos realized the need for a calvary troop in the fight against the Persians so that it would not be necessary for him to wage war as though he were running away. The Greek word for running away, *drapeteuonta*,[11] connotes a slave deserting. Xenophon could not have intimated Agesilaos' free nobility more succinctly.

It is not surprising, therefore, given Xenophon's taste for the right word at the right time, his sense of definition so to speak, that he should also show a penchant for specifically technical terms. The mind which could produce a professional treatise on horsemanship desired always and everywhere to call a thing by its exact name.[12] Thus Xenophon calls the ruler of Thessaly *tagos*, the Thessalian term, whereas Herodotos and Thucydides before him had used the more familiar gloss *basileus*. He does not like the vague and the general; he will not say "magistrate" when he can say "ephor," and he is therefore not adverse to using non-Attic and even non-Greek vocabulary to give his writing an authentic, and incidentally cosmopolitan, air.

But words by themselves are only the beginning; they open to a larger perspective. Xenophon's concern for individual words naturally evolves into a concern for the individual details of a scene which seem to manifest themselves spontaneously even as Xenophon consciously focuses them into coherent unity. It is no small token of his skill that, perhaps as a direct result of his respect for the particular, Xenophon tends to view events not from the outside but from within, from the point of view of those involved in them.[13] An ancient critic confirms the worthiness of the following passage; its excellence remains instructive:

> καὶ ἐνταῦθα δὴ φύρδην ἐμάχοντο καὶ πεζοὶ καὶ ἱππεῖς, πεπτωκὼς δέ τις ὑπὸ τῷ Κύρου ἵππῳ καὶ πατούμενος παίει εἰς τὴν γαστέρα τῇ μαχαίρᾳ τὸν ἵππον αὐτοῦ· ὁ δὲ ἵππος πληγεὶς σφαδάζων ἀποσείεται τὸν Κῦρον.

> And there indeed were they fighting in utter confusion, both foot and cavalry, and one man, having fallen beneath Cyrus'

horse and being trampled, strikes at the belly of the horse with his sabre. But the horse, stabbed, rearing up, unseats Cyrus.[14]

It should now go without saying that the man strikes not with any "weapon," but with a sabre, and that the horse rears up in the Greek with a word which is the precise term for the jerking of a bronco being broken, so excruciating is its pain. Of equal interest, however, is the way Xenophon's description proceeds in the manner the man's own mind must have responded to his situation. Thus it is the "belly" that comes next in its clause after the verb "strikes," since it is the immediate reaction of the man first to strike and then to strike at what he immediately sees closest, which from his vantage is the horse's underside. The electrifying effect on the horse is also well caught when Xenophon lists without connective the two participles and the climactic verb, the three words following on the page, just as the events they describe follow in immediate succession upon one another in deed. Xenophon's prose moves as fast as the action.

Xenophon's ability to build from the particular word and detail to a general effect can also be seen in the following passage from the *Hellenika*, in which he creates a sense of urgency and suspense by the careful arrangement of significant features:

> ἱππεύς τις προσήλαυνε καὶ μάλα ἰσχυρῶς ἱδρῶντι τῷ ἵππῳ. ὑπὸ πολλῶν δὲ ἐρωτώμενος ὅτι ἀγγέλλοι, οὐδενὶ ἀπεκρίνατο, ἀλλ' ἐπειδὴ ἐγγὺς ἦν τοῦ Ἀγησιλάου, καθαλόμενος ἀπὸ τοῦ ἵππου καὶ προσδραμὼν αὐτῷ μάλα σκυθρωπὸς ὢν λέγει τὸ τῆς ἐν Λεχαίῳ μόρας πάθος.
>
> And a rider galloped up with his horse dripping sweat. When many asked him what the news was, he answered no one; but when he was near Agesilaos, having leapt from his horse and run up to him, with a gloomy look, he tells him the Lechaion company's disaster.[15]

Xenophon does not obtrusively manipulate the narration here but lets the events of the scene speak for themselves. The sweating horse, the rider's failure to respond to queries, and his mournful countenance just before he speaks all add to the feeling of increasing apprehension without Xenophon's ever saying in so many words that something critical has happened or that people in the Spartan army are anxious. The reader goes through the action as the action naturally unfolds itself, he experiences it with Xenophon just as the actual persons involved may be thought to have experienced it. And his sense of terrible disaster is reinforced all the more by Xenophon's keeping back the crucial word *pathos* until the very last possible moment, when the climax of this small drama is attained and the tension relaxed.

Xenophon's power to engage his reader owes more than a little to persistent avoidance of the majestic and the self-important. Even in perhaps the most famous scene in all his works, the Ten Thousand's sighting of the sea, he maintains a calm sense of what went on; and in the midst of all the excitement, he can even take time to mention the name of a fellow cavalryman, Lykios, who rides with him to the van of the army to investigate the cries. And all that he hears is one word, repeated, "the sea! the sea!" and all that he sees is the men embracing one another and weeping.[16] No disquisitions on the feeling of relief or elaborations on the sense of joy, no flamboyant rhetoric. Just one word and a few telling details suffice for a memorable effect. It is an intense climax, undiffuse.

But once again Xenophon is not only capable of such achievement when writing about the exciting or thrilling. His powerful simplicity can also be moving in more quiet ways. In the *Kyroupaideia* he relates how Pantheia, the wife of Abrodatas, presents her husband with new armor she has made for him herself. Addressing him as he goes forth to what will be a fatal battle,

> ἐνέδυε τὰ ὅπλα, καὶ λανθάνειν μὲν ἐπειρᾶτο, ἐλείβετο δὲ αὐτῇ τὰ δάκρυα κατὰ τῶν παρειῶν.
>
> she put the armor on him and tried to avoid notice, but down dropped the tears upon her cheeks.[17]

Xenophon of course articulates the sentence so that the important verbs receive due emphasis from their position, but he also manages to hold back the tears in the phrase even as the weeping woman tries to restrain them. He also sees fit, moreover, to add as a final delicate detail "upon her cheeks," not only to give the sentence an attractive falling action, bringing it to a gentle finish, but also to leave the reader with an image finely wrought and much more telling than if he had commented at length about the woman's inner state. He has made the interior visible: what is so palpable has no need of commentary. Though written apropos of the *Anabasis*, Hippolyte Taine's remarks on Xenophon's style suit all of Xenophon's works. Xenophon's narrative, he said, is the "pure reflection of occurrences"; and if an image were to be sought to express the style of Xenophon, "one would have to compare it to the water of a brook upon leaving its source, still without admixture, light and limpid, more beautiful than when it will be sullied and troubled by the progress of its course."[18]

As any reader of Xenophon will confirm, Xenophon was interested in that kind of political, military, and financial economy which accomplishes as much as possible however small the resources. His own technique of writing consequently seems to bear witness to a more pervasive state of mind, for his use of words certainly seeks to obtain much with the least amount of verbal expenditure. Never pugnacious, never straining, Xenophon's style proceeds from the realization that less is more. This is not to deny, of course, that Xenophon uses conventional figures or that he can wax overtly rhetorical. But when he does so, it is never for mere show or embellishment.[19] He is always concerned to do what is proper and suitable for his ends and not to exceed this limit. Above all his considered choice of words and simple syntax aim at presenting every object, every expression as concretely and precisely as possible so that nothing intervenes between the observer and the observed. Xenophon essentially turns outside of himself to the object; simply as a stylist he is engaged in a constant process of definition by which he sets his careful limits around something in order better to know it. Quietly but continually he analyzes and reduces things to their essence, as if seeking to answer, on the most basic level, the question "what is?" His very method of writing implies a continuing search for fundamental order.

Though it will always be impossible to determine exactly why a man writes as he does, perhaps it will not be too fanciful to see in Xenophon the stylist a reflection of Xenophon the Socratic. Within the context of a philosophy which stresses the importance of the exact definition of things and the answer to the ongoing search for "what is," it is readily understandable that Xenophon should often employ the exact name of a thing rather than a synonym and that he should be concerned with precise description of an action.[20] Such are the mechanics of his realism and the moving force behind his simple and lucid sentence structures. The involved and overwrought antitheses of Thucydides and the rich but cloying flow of Isokrates have been reduced to an exquisite vivacity. Only the essential matters; anything else is cosmetic, false appearance rather than true reality.

Yet it would be a mistake to see in Xenophon's realism anything approaching a mean-spirited fastidiousness or a striving after naturalistic effect.[21] For the intriguing mystery of his style is the way it can so fully convey what it says so sparingly, refusing to be obvious or to spell things out. To borrow Taine's assessment, Xenophon's manner is intrinsically imagistic, not just because it attempts to describe, but because it invites a closer gaze which reveals to reflective scrutiny more than at first glance seemed to be there. Even in something as relatively unimportant as the tears on Pantheia's cheeks there is a suggestion of more than a simple and momentary sadness, and in the cry "the sea!" more is involved than an uncomplicated joy at a sighting.[22] At the risk of outraging paradox, it can be said that Xenophon's methodical insistence on definition, far from closing in the possible range of view,[23] broadens it to the point where it can almost touch in freedom the multiple intangibles of things in themselves.

Just as it was a rash man who thought he had a ready answer for every one of Socrates' questions, it would be a rash man who thought he could understand Xenophon in a trice. The clarity of Socrates' student does not stress the obvious and trite, and the one who reads him must be careful to appreciate both his words and especially their context, if he is to avoid misinterpretation. Xenophon's style invites the reader to look—and to keep on looking. Unfortunately modern scholars rarely do this, who come to Xenophon all too often expecting a straightforward recital of events such as they themselves might produce in a text or a lecture.[24] It will be appropriate therefore to investigate the variety of Xenophon's artistry a little further.

Take, for example, the famous speech of Kallias at the first peace conference of 371:

> Ὦ ἄνδρες Λακεδαιμόνιοι, τὴν μὲν προξενίαν ὑμῶν οὐκ ἐγὼ μόνος, ἀλλὰ καὶ πατρὸς πατὴρ πατρῴαν ἔχων παρεδίδου τῷ γένει.
>
> Men of Lacedaemon, it is not only I who possess your proxeny, but my father's father, possessing it as a paternal inheritance, passed it on in the family.[25]

More than one reader has noted the rhetoric of this speech in general and the heavy alliteration of p-sounds with which it commences. It assaults the ear; the effect is obvious and heavy. It is just the opposite, in other words, of Xenophon's normal manner. But he has previously introduced the speaker as a man who was no less pleased at being praised by himself than by others.[26] What Xenophon has done is both to characterize the man talking with the man's own words and to have a joke at his expense. Kallias' inflated rhetoric bursts its own bubble. Elsewhere in the *Hellenika* Xenophon expresses admiration for the way Iphikrates was able to train his troops simultaneously for sailing and fighting.[27] In speeches, especially, he himself achieves an analogous economy by letting speech, as here with Kallias, be dramatic: how people speak reveals them for what they are. It thus becomes even more difficult, it goes without saying, to determine just where Xenophon's own sentiments truly lie.

What weight, for instance, is to be placed on the strong word *hubreōs* (insolence) when the Spartans deliberate about the advisability of waging a war against the Thebans?

> They reckoned that it was a fine opportunity for leading forth an army against them and for putting an end to the Thebans' insolence towards them.[28]

Is Xenophon vouching for the *hubris* of the Thebans? He may, quite to the contrary, be presenting the Spartan side of the question and implying nothing about the accuracy of the

Spartan assessment. This same sort of crucial discernment must above all be made when statements in one context seem to be connected with what may in fact be genuine beliefs of Xenophon as he expresses them in other portions of his works. In the *Anabasis* the gruff Spartan Klearkhos delivers a speech to the mendacious Tissaphernes, seeking to allay suspicions between the Greeks and the Persians after Kounaxa.[29] He begins with a lesson in theology on the sacredness of oaths such as the Greeks and Persians had already sworn, averring that no man can escape from the gods if he prevaricates, that there is no place, no fortress, no darkness to which he might hie him, for the gods see everything and rule everything.[30] One commentator on this text remarks that its sophistic artifices of style are a rare eloquence for a Spartan, especially since it was all being wasted on someone who did not know Greek. He can only see an example of Xenophon's readiness to moralize.[31] Now Xenophon may have been a pious man (and there is little reason to think him otherwise),[32] but this need not be the explanation of Klearkhos' words. Xenophon has previously shown Klearkhos engaged in religious activity,[33] and he has also made it clear that the Spartan has not been as successful as he might have wished in extricating the Ten Thousand from their predicament after Kounaxa.[34] Perhaps Klearkhos' piety is a piety *in extremis*. Be that as it may, his loquacity and rhetoric on the matter of the gods are not so much Xenophon's moralizing as Klearkhos' own attempt to impress Tissaphernes with Greek fidelity; for the Greeks at this stage had little else to impress with, and what could be more impressive than the gods, no matter whether or not Klearkhos' belief was abiding and sincere? Klearkhos' unlaconic disquisition is not an intrusion of the author's personality but a further manifestation through the dramatic use of speech of a particular man's response to a difficult situation.

Another Spartan in difficulties was the admiral Kallikratidas, who succeeded Lysander in the command of the Ionian front during the last years of the Peloponnesian War.[35] In fact his troubles began because his predecessor was far more capable than he. Kallikratidas' inadequacy became even more clear, especially to his allies, when, like Lysander before him, he had to secure funds from the younger Cyrus.[36] Lysander, showing patience and wit, had charmed the money out of Cyrus.[37] Not so Kallikratidas:

> angered at the put-off and the standings around at the door, he said in a rage that the Greeks were most pitiful because they had to wheedle barbarians for money; and he continued by saying that, if he got home safe, he would stop, with all the power he had, the Athenians and the Spartans from warring against one another. He then sailed away to Miletos.[38]

Taking this passage at face value, some readers assert it is a key text expressing Xenophon's alleged sympathy with the Isokratean notion of an anti-Persian panhellenism.[39] But they have neglected to observe, first of all, that Kallikratidas speaks in anger and so not with what even he may have considered good sense, and, secondly, that he lacks just the intelligent verve Xenophon admired and could see in Lysander. It is hard to imagine Xenophon expressing his own views through a boor, no matter what he believed about panhellenism. Furthermore the whole context of Kallikratidas' command should be considered before making a judgment about his exalted sense of international politics. Xenophon records that shortly after Kallikratidas went off in a pet to Miletos, he captured Methymna and refused to let his captives be sold into slavery, proclaiming grandly that as long as he was in command *(heatou ge arkhontos)*, no Greek was going to be enslaved if he could help it.[40] Yet the very next day he surrenders over to slavery the Athenian garrison there, conveniently forgetting both that they are Greeks and that he once viewed himself as a peacemaker between Athens and Sparta.[41] He is, in short, a man whose only consistency lies in his quick ability to turn a phrase to insure his own sense of superiority and to balm his own hurt pride. Never at a loss, as soon as he has settled affairs in Methymna, he declares that he will stop Konon the Athenian from fornicating the sea *(moikhōnta tēn thalattan)*.[42] He is given here quite simply the most startling image in the entire corpus of Xenophon but his audacity finds its quelling in a relief fleet this very Konon cleverly secures. At Arginousai he meets a fate ironically befitting a Spartan—drowning.[43] Those, therefore, who see in Kallikratidas a sympathetic appeal for Greek brotherhood may find themselves instead the object of Xenophon's own parody.

The example of Kallikratidas reveals an important facet of Xenophon's method of writing. The Spartan's words and his actions do not jibe, and Xenophon invites the reader to make this realization by letting what happened speak for itself. There develops a silent tension between the author and the agent, between the one speaking at a given moment and the other writing continuously. Xenophon rarely states outright what ought to be the reaction to an event or a speech, and from this unwillingness to say too much he creates a tug between what is apparently being said and what is actually the case. This discrepancy between appearance and reality is the source of Xenophon's ironic humor. But its operation is not always so simple as in the case of Kallikratidas. It is revealing, for instance, to find Xenophon in one of his relatively infrequent personal comments making a point of admiring the wit of Theramenes. Theramenes at his execution, it will be remembered, poured a toast with the fatal hemlock "to the beautiful Kritias" who had secured his condemnation:

> ... but I judge this admirable in the man, that when death was at hand he lost neither his sense nor his sense of humor.[44]

Likewise it is Xenophon who reports in the *Apology* an especially ironic remark of Socrates before his death. The well-meaning but simpleminded Apollodoros cried for Socrates because he was so unjustly convicted. "Would you prefer, dear Apollodoros, to see me dying justly rather than unjustly?" And Socrates laughed as he spoke.[45]

Xenophon's irony is more than dramatic. The jokes made by Theramenes and Socrates before death reveal not so much an opposition between what they say and what they think or what is actually the case, as an opposition between what they say and what they perceive to be the inherent nature of things. Socrates and Theramenes are both beyond the point of caring about hitting back at their judges or achieving a forensic victory. Their manner of expression emanates instead from their perception of a fundamental antagonism between what appears and what is real, what seems to be important and what genuinely is so. Their words become playful because words, at least in their cases, have previously failed to establish what they think is their justice, to say "what is." Yet it is only in their playfulness that Theramenes and Socrates achieve a liberation from their absurd situations and in fact obtain a triumph even as they lose. Thus irony, if just for a moment, bridges the gap between appearance and reality in the only way possible. It merely and delightfully turns the tables, for by saying "what is not" it allusively summons forth "what is." Xenophon, in an intriguing passage, remarks on the beauty of ordered arrangements but points out that what is left untouched around them also contributes to their beauty, like the empty space a circular chorus maintains in its center as it dances.[46] It is this pure and unarticulated region wherein irony dwells, adding another and important dimension to the verbal choreography which shapes it and makes it visible.

Irony is also, therefore, self-effacing, and the ironic man, to the Greeks at any rate, was someone who claimed to have less than he actually did.[47] There was a contrast, for example, between Socrates' knowledge and his profession of ignorance. But, as Socrates knew, there may come a point when this discrepancy ceases to be illusory; and so Aristotle can say that the ironic man is not untruthful.[48] He is by no means, as Aristotle further makes clear, an *alazōn*, a man who boasts, who claims to have more than he actually does.[49] The ironic man is thus more attractive and charming because he speaks not for gain but to avoid bombast.[50] Irony shuns exaggeration and is the fitting companion of the unpretentious and the simple.

The ironic mode suits Xenophon's style well; indeed, it is an essential part of that style, just as articulated space and empty space cannot be separated in the dance. Xenophon seems especially interested in defining things not by the piling up of rigid details but by a careful choice of words and aspects which, by their ordered placement in a context, come to imply more than their "first meaning." Irony, too, proceeds by implication, but its good sense keeps it from vacuous abstraction, just as Xenophon's sense of words keeps him joyfully content with the concrete. His use of irony, in fact, suggests a further refinement of his verbal sense, namely, that no matter how carefully chosen words are, they cannot reproduce exactly what they describe. So the less said the better, for perhaps only by keeping to the down-to-earth will the nature of things be revealed.

If Xenophon's use of irony was naturally appropriate, it was also to be expected because he was a student of Socrates. But if Xenophon's simple style can be said in some sense to reflect a Socratic influence, so too can his infusion of that style with irony. "Socratic irony, at its center, expresses the tension between ignorance—that is, the impossibility ultimately to put into words 'what justice is'—and the direct experience of the unknown, the existence of the just man. . . ."[51] Xenophon's appreciation of this tension was, of course, most fully realized in his understanding of Socrates himself. Socrates was for him the most perfect of men, who embodied, if he could not finally define, all those virtues which were most noble in life.[52] Xenophon also maintained that Socrates was both a serious and a playful man,[53] and it is these two aspects which irony seems to fuse. Irony becomes an essential element of the Socratic outlook because the concern for what is most important can humanly only be satisfied through a jesting and sporting encounter with the world of appearance. Needless to say, this attitude is not comprehensible to all, and not all men understand the requirements of irony; Socrates' own fate testifies to the unfortunate blindness of others. Irony is also the means by which the man concerned with what really is maintains his fidelity to the truth when speaking to the vulgar.[54] It preserves and protects, as well as expresses, the individual awareness of what matters most of all.

Irony gives nothing away, but it does invite those who observe it to look and look again. It thus sheds a further grace and deeper beauty on Xenophon's descriptive charms.

For what could be more pleasing than the moment when, all of a sudden and quite unexpectedly, the reader is led to discover where appearance passes into reality and style, by a mental economy, is changed into substance?

In no other work did Xenophon display his concern and appreciation for the importance of humor and irony more than in the *Symposium*, and it is this work which will best introduce and demonstrate his habits of mind as they operate on a larger scale. Few commentators have failed to enjoy its ingratiating allure and its amusing *politesse*.[55] But the further implications of its stated theme of *paidia*, playfulness,[56] have rarely been appreciated.

A symposium was ostensibly a gathering of friends in search of a good time. It was something informal, where conversation was supposed to be free and impromptu; and since all were among friends, it was not surprising that the talk should turn to amatory themes.[57] In fact Xenophon elsewhere remarks that Socrates' love was related to his playfulness, because, though he frequently said he loved somebody, it was clear that he loved not beautiful bodies but beautiful souls.[58] This playfulness could go to apparently outrageous extremes; so that when Socrates was invited to Kallias' house, Xenophon records he asserted he was more beautiful than another guest, the young and handsome Kritoboulos.[59] A beauty contest was even held, conducted like a mock trial, which Socrates unfortunately did not win, since under the artificial lamplight of the party Kritoboulos' physical beauty outshone the dumpiness of Socrates' body.[60]

Kritoboulos is not the only man against whom Socrates is thrown in gentle opposition at dinner. His very presence at Kallias' house in the first place is something of an anomaly; for the men have only met by chance, and Kallias is a known supporter of the sophists.[61] The Syracusan entertainer whom Kallias has hired also speaks out nastily against Socrates, being chagrined at the philosopher's disinclination for his troupe's act,[62] while the comedian Philip vies with Socrates in raising laughs.[63] On the other hand, Hermogenes, a rather sanctimonious and utterly witless fellow, bridles when Socrates tries to amend his sourness,[64] although he can indeed praise Socrates at one point for charming and instructing Kallias all at once. Since it is just this charm Hermogenes lacks, his compliment to Socrates, though sincere, is leaden.[65] Perhaps even more deficient in charm and a sense of the appropriate is Antisthenes, who has the boldness to claim that his wealth is far superior to his host Kallias', because it is interior, and that he is quite content with an external poverty which permits him always to be with Socrates.[66] Socrates, however, is not fooled; and he can say, with ever a smile, that Antisthenes is in love, not with his soul, but with his lovely body.[67] Antisthenes is the quintessential crank who likes deprivation because it gives him something to boast about. He is, let it be said, an *alazōn*, and his own words about his riches may contain more truth than he himself would care to realize.[68]

Antisthenes is a fundamentally unfriendly man; and it is not uncharacteristic to find him, during the discussion of what those at the party think most valuable, ready to pounce petulantly on anybody else's ideas which seem to him deficient. He assaults Kallias' notion that money, amply distributed, will make men just of itself, and he belittles Nikeratos' belief in the ultimate value of Homer for leading a good life.[69] It is always Socrates who restrains Antisthenes from committing more social *faux pas*, since a party is hardly the place for cross examinations.[70] Socrates' sense of grace, in other words, seems to lead him to manifest his sense of friendship, a friendship both for Antisthenes, whom he stops from doing what is wrong, and for the others, who might soon become Antisthenes' victims and finally his enemies. Socrates is the peacemaker.

But he certainly has a sizeable task before him, since all too few of his partners at dinner are disposed to be really friendly. Even Kritoboulos, who is madly in love with the handsome Kleinias, describes his love as though it were something exclusive, in which the rest of the world does not figure, indeed does not matter, because all that is important is the private mutual gratification of himself and his beloved.[71] Kallias, the host, shows himself from the first to be incredibly pompous, and his words and actions in his own home seem no less aimed at his self-satisfaction than will his remarks later in his life to the public assembly at Sparta. His love for Autolykos, the young, prize-winning athlete in whose honor he is giving the party, is infatuation with a new ornament. Hermogenes is so friendly with the gods that Socrates says a man must be thankful that he continues to associate with mortals.[72] Nikeratos, though newly married,[73] puts more store in his Homer than in his wife, while the Syracusan prays to the gods in hardly altruistic fashion that they always supply him with empty-headed people to enjoy his brainless productions.[74] The comedian Philip is a merciless mimic and parodist,[75] and it is his uninvited entrance which dispels the force of love originally exerted over the company by the presence of Autolykos.[76] Then there is Kharmides whose remarks contain a thinly disguised vitriol when he, as a foil to Antisthenes, defends poverty as the best thing in life.[77] Having lost his wealth because of the city's war and taxes, he is finally let alone to do just what he wants; and he claims to be just like a tyrant, where before he was practically a slave.[78] Now Kharmides' jest about being a tyrant is no laughing matter, for he became, in fact, one of the Thirty and was implicated in the murder of his fellow guest Nikeratos and the confiscation of that man's wealth.[79]

Dinner at Kallias' thus becomes more and more sinister. At an affair where friendship should grow, it gradually appears that it is more a case of hostility being repressed. Only Socrates displays a continual awareness of what is fitting, and only he manages occasionally to get some people to do the right thing. Antisthenes can be checked, as can Philip, and even the Syracusan can be moved to put on a more appropriate act than his troupe's previous feats of juggling and derring-do.[80] It is also Socrates who gets everyone to laugh when he proclaims that he values most highly in life the matchmaker's occupation.[81] Socrates' business is the procurer's love trade, the introduction of people to what best suits them and will best make them happy. He alone in the *Symposium*, moreover, talks at length about love, insisting that it is to this god that all the company are in thrall.[82]

Thus he is the true master of ceremonies, who provides the true entertainment, and his entertainment economically accomplishes, as Hermogenes finds it necessary to observe, the further end of enlightenment and education. The many facets of Socratic playfulness consequently reveal themselves and their interconnectedness. *Paidia* achieves *paideia* for Socrates' beloved, his *paidika*.

For in his discourse on love, in which he says that he does not know a time when he was not in love with somebody,[83] he gives a lesson to all his companions about all the things which they have previously said. He interprets Homer for Nikeratos,[84] he refutes Kritoboulos' assertion that lovers are the best comrades-in-arms,[85] he makes a proper comparison for Philip,[86] he praises the god of graceful love for Hermogenes,[87] tells Antisthenes about love of the soul,[88] and disposes of Kallias' theory that money alone will make men better.[89] But the real thrust of his speech is to make the others, and especially Kallias, understand the liberating nature of "heavenly love" and the debasement of "vulgar love," to make them aware that the love of friends leads men outside of themselves to an increasingly improving society wherein mutual sharing of virtue leads to virtue's greatest possible increase.[90] For a man will only retain the friendship of the noble and good *(kalos kagathos)* if he is concerned with *aretē*, while love of the body is essentially unfriendly and unsocial, because it is really concerned with self-gratification. Socrates thus also reveals his civic nature, since his praise of love's virtue becomes an inducement, as Kallias realizes,[91] to noble enterprise outside the self for the city; and Socrates can state that he has ever been with the city a fellow lover *(sunerastēs)* of those good by nature who zealously strive for excellence.[92]

Socrates' talk has gradually elevated the discussion of the *Symposium* to a serious level, but it remains lighthearted, if only because Socrates compliments his companions and assumes the best about them.[93] Socrates' seriousness and his humor finally come together; and in so doing they cast a spell with their splendid vision, so that Lykon, Autolykos' father and a man of few words, can say to Socrates:

Νὴ τὴν Ἥραν, ὦ Σώκρατες, καλός γε κἀγαθὸς δοκεῖς μοι ἄνθρωπος εἶναι.

By Hera, Socrates, you seem to me to be an exceedingly noble and good person.[94]

But Lykon was one of those who accused Socrates and obtained his execution.[95] Socrates ultimately fails to convince all who hear him, no matter how persuasive he is. Just as he loses the mock beauty trial to Kritoboulos, so he will lose the real trial for his life. Not everyone will listen to him, just as at the dinner Philip succeeds, despite Socrates, in having the servants pour the wine rather too freely.[96] And even when Socrates attempts to establish the honor of matchmaking,[97] some participants fail to pay attention, as they show at one point by giving an inappropriate reply which momentarily derails the argument.[98] Finally the Syracusan returns at the *Symposium's* end to put on a more fitting entertainment, a masque of Bacchus and Ariadne, which has the effect of making the married guests leap on their horses to be off to their wives and the nonmarried vow that they soon will wed.[99] The spell of Socrates has been forgotten.

If the *Symposium* is basically about play, love, and the society of friends and the city, the sad truth emerges that the joke is on Socrates. Confronted at Kallias' with devotees of the sophists and comedy, fathers and sons, tyrants and the pious,[100] Socrates exerts a sway which is momentary though real enough. But Socrates always knows that he is probably attempting the very arduous, just as he knows that endeavor is safe only if the god does not interfere.[101] Nonetheless he continues to charm those with whom he comes in contact, in a way they rarely ever fully understand.[102] For he calls them peacefully and playfully to a better sense of themselves, a sense which unfortunately few are willing to entertain when sobered up in what they might consider the harshness of the real world.

Xenophon's *Symposium* embodies all that charming wit and keen appreciation for the appropriate which are the token of Xenophon's style. And like Xenophon's style, the *Symposium* builds upon a clear perception of a situation which is so described as to lead to the awareness that there is more to something than its surface. The careful characterizations of Kallias' dinner guests and their amusing contretemps will always delight in themselves, but the reader who stops there will rather resemble Antisthenes, who loved a true, but external, form of Socrates, because he did not see through to Socrates' soul. Xenophon's grace is not superficial, nor is his humor unrefined; like those of Socrates, they dwell within, each playing upon the other, each masked by irony, each never spoiled by the coarseness and sorrow their creator knew too well.

At the end of his party, Kallias walks out with Autolykos to the young victor's exercises.[103] Socrates follows along, doubtless seeking once again to fall under the effect of Autolykos' beauty which he felt at the party's beginning. Not everyone else goes with Socrates, but Xenophon, a guest like the others, could have been among them.[104] He does not say so, for that is his way. Perhaps he thought the *Symposium* spoke for him.

2

SOCRATES

Defenceless under the night
Our world in stupour lies;
Yet, dotted everywhere,
Ironic points of light
Flash out wherever the Just
Exchange their messages:
May I, composed like them
Of Eros and of dust,
Beleaguered by the sáme
Negation and despair
Show an affirming flame.
                —W.H. Auden

Handsome, wealthy, and bright, Xenophon must still have thought the world was his that day when Socrates first met him. The old man had an eye for talent and character; and, skilled examiner that he was, he could not have put to Xenophon a better question to interest and confound him all at once. "Where could the necessities of life be bought?" he asked him; and Xenophon, that lover of order, knew precisely where each thing could be obtained. But when asked where men became noble and good, he was at a loss and confused. He found a way out of his ignorance by becoming an adherent of the poor and ugly philosopher.[1]

The effect of the relationship on Xenophon was profound. In everything he wrote, it has justly been observed,[2] the mark of Socrates can be seen; the dominant influence of his intellectual life was the power exerted by this unique individual. Some modern commentators, however, spellbound by Plato and unsympathetic to Xenophon's Socratic works, have wondered whether he was, in fact, a real disciple of Plato's master or whether he was instead an "outsider,"[3] who had constantly to assert his claim of admission into the inner circle of genuine followers. But antiquity was never in doubt, nor should modernity muse, especially when it has finally been realized that the quest for the historical Socrates in the accounts of Socratics must end nowhere, since accurate history was never their concern. The impact of an individual was what mattered.

Yet though Xenophon often heard and admired Socrates, he did not always heed him. Eager to leave Athens and be off to Asia Minor and the camp of Cyrus, he sought his teacher's advice and was told to ask the counsel of the Delphic god. But the impetuous young man asked not whether, but how, he might best go.[4] His life was thus changed forever, since his absence was to last longer than he expected. Born an Athenian, he would be condemned to live many of his mature years in exile.

Of his exile, as of his life, little is known, much is speculated. Diogenes Laertios is the principal source, and Wilamowitz has not found him wanting.[5] But Diogenes offers a sketch, not a portrait; and it is unfortunate that on the question of Xenophon's banishment he is less than conclusive. He offers two reasons and one date; Xenophon was exiled in 399 either for joining Cyrus' expedition or for laconism in surrendering over to Agesilaos the remnants of the Ten Thousand.[6] Scholars have found much to fault in this account and are as ready to impugn Diogenes' date as they are his conflicting presentation of the charge. Accordingly many have changed the year to 394 to preserve the exile for laconism, since in that year Xenophon offered clear proof of treasonable activity when he accompanied the Spartans into battle against the Athenians at Koroneia. Furthermore it is impossible that any Athenian could have been exiled for laconism in 399, since Athens contributed a cavalry troop to the same force the Ten Thousand joined,[7] and because Athens was at that time part of the Spartan hegemony established by Lysander. On this the Oxyrynchos Historian is clear, for he describes the great and constant effort made by those in control at Athens in this period to smooth over hostility to the city's master.[8]

Yet it should be noted that Diogenes makes a mistake when he presents the charge as laconism, and so maybe he has erred in a more crucial way. He says that Xenophon handed over the Ten Thousand to Agesilaos, when in fact it was Thibron's force he joined in 399.[9] The 399 date for Xenophon's exile deserves more respect, not that it has been without its supporters, amongst whom must be reckoned the only other ancient witnesses, Pausanias[10] and Dio Chrysostom.[11] Xenophon merited exile, it is suggested, because Cyrus was an ally of Sparta during the Peloponnesian War who also meant to usurp the throne of Artaxerxes who was a friend of Athens. Xenophon, therefore, was not banished overtly for laconism but for a lack of patriotism manifested in his aiding another enemy. But Grote's criticism of this view is telling, since he correctly points out that Artaxerxes did not become a friend of Athens until 396 at the earliest and that in 399 Artaxerxes was just as much an enemy of Athens as Cyrus was.[12] To connect 399 and Cyrus by arguing that collaboration with the Persian was the official and ostensible charge and laconism the real, though hidden, one does not escape the dilemma.[13] A condemnation implying laconism would certainly have offended the Spartans little less than a charge more openly expressed.

Perhaps the text of Xenophon may afford a solution. The only work in which the exile is mentioned is the *Anabasis*, and it would not seem unreasonable to suggest some connection exists between the two. When Socrates was asked by his young friend about joining the expedition, he was clearly hesitant to advise it.[14] The sense of foreboding here is increased later in the work when Xenophon gives a lengthy description of his estate in Skillous where he actually spent his exile[15] and by his outright assertion, still further on, that a vote had not yet been taken against him in Athens about exile.[16] The use of the expression "not yet" makes an exile some five years after the context, that is, in 394, seem unlikely.[17] Sometime soon after the narrative setting, that is, in 399, would be more probable.

A reason remains to be found; and if the year is 399, it cannot have anything to do with laconism. It should also be remembered that the courts were busy that year, and prosecutions on trumped-up charges were not unheard of. Andokides and Socrates were both tried then, the accusations against the latter obvious fabrications. Andokides had been in trouble ever since he had allegedly profaned the Mysteries with Alkibiades; and few would deny that Socrates' real undoing was his association with Alkibiades and others, especially Kritias, who were involved in, and held responsible for, Athens' defeat in the Peloponnesian War or for the excesses of the tyranny of the Thirty. Upon their teacher's execution, Plato and other Socratics fled Athens for Megara, knowing a hostile environment when they saw one and not wishing, doubtless, to provoke prosecutions against themselves. Xenophon was not to be so lucky. Perhaps tainted by an association not only with Socrates but also with the oligarchs,[18] he fell victim to the Athenian democrats' ability to forgive but not forget.[19] He gave an excuse for indictment by his association with Cyrus, an old foe of the city; but in reality he suffered the consequence of politically unfortunate associations centered in Athens itself and having nothing to do primarily with Sparta. Yet while Athenian exile would presage future disfavor, youthful imprudence would be tempered to philosophy.

Xenophon's condemnation may or may not have been justified, but like Socrates he did experience firsthand the force of Athenian law.[20] There was never any doubt, however, that Socrates was guiltless; and his execution by the city clearly revolutionized the lives of some of his followers, most notably Xenophon and Plato,[21] and forced them to reconsider their relation to Athens. The injustice Socrates suffered made even more urgent the need to answer a question he himself had been fond of asking, namely, "what is justice?" But since justice seemed to include the notion of the legal and the regulation of men's affairs, it immediately involved another and still more basic question, the definition of the city. Furthermore Socrates' followers were also eager to exonerate their master both against the accusations made at his trial and against the attacks made by fourth-century sophists like Polykrates.[22] So a writer of talent like Xenophon had a ready invitation to connect with the immediate desire for rebuttal the investigation of deeper issues which would enable him to bring the justification of Socrates back to first principles and to effect a refutation of all charges, not just particular points. Accordingly the *Memorabilia*, which is structured like a classic defense speech,[23] can be seen as Xenophon's statement of Socrates' justice; and as the title suggests, Socrates' justice was Xenophon's principal memory. That is to say, Xenophon's central interest in his Socratic heritage was with the question of civic life and its functioning. This is also apparent in the *Oikonomikos* and the *Apology* which, though they do not specifically attempt to justify Socrates, nevertheless seek to establish clearly, by investigating from angles different from that of the *Memorabilia*, the nature of the Socratic life and the connection between the philosopher and the city. There is then a unity to Xenophon's appreciation of Socrates which begins and ends with the *polis*.[24]

Socrates once had a conversation with the hedonist Aristippos from which Xenophon saw a fundamental lesson emerge.[25] Continuing a theme of the first book of the *Memorabilia*, Xenophon has Socrates ask his partner about the necessity for self-control *(enkrateia)* in matters of diet, sex, and physical conditioning in the education of those meant to rule and those not meant to. The conversation is thus not about self-control in itself but about its civic dimension.[26] Only those with the ability to endure toils and who do not lead the soft life can qualify as rulers, for only they have managed to rule themselves. The progression is important: individual mastery is the basis of societal mastery.

Aristippos, upon Socrates' questioning, confesses that he has no desire to be a ruler and that he has the better lot because he is spared the pains of office. Yet when Socrates compels him to admit that rulers live better than ruled, he understands the price of slavery but attempts to escape the dilemma by maintaining that there is a third option, a *via media* between ruler and slave, which is the radical freedom of the man who does not "lock himself up in a polity but is a stranger *(xenos)* everywhere."[27] Socrates, however, points out that this is only another form of slavery and worse than the last, since injustice inevitably victimizes it. The stranger on the road is the easy prey of wrongdoers, and he can have no city's laws to turn to for protection or redress.[28] Aristippos' way is impossible for a man; the individual must be in the *polis*. The argument has thus reversed itself: the individual now needs society, whereas before he needed to be its ruler. Xenophon establishes, in other words, that, contrary to the sophists, the individual is not radically autonomous and that the *polis* is inherent in human nature. He looks forward to Aristotle's famous formulation that man is the political animal and that he who is without a state is either a bad man or above humanity.[29]

Xenophon concludes Socrates' conversation with Aristippos by recounting in Socrates' words Prodikos' famous parable about Herakles' choice of either the way of Vice or the way of Virtue. Two options are open, there is no middle way, and the individual is responsible for the choice he must make.[30] But even as the story sums up the gist of the preceding exchange, it also makes clear one further point. The way of Vice is the way of the solitary man, the way of Virtue is the way of the social man. As Virtue tells Vice for Herakles' profit, she associates with the gods and good men, and through her men are dear to the gods, loved by their friends, and honored by their country; but Vice, though immortal, travels abroad, expelled from the company of the gods and trusted by no one.[31] The life of toil and honor to which Virtue invites Herakles thus seems to be the only true life for a man, and the self-control which Socrates recommended to Aristippos turns out to be not only the requirement of the man who will rule but of man pure and simple; it is not for nothing that Socrates uses similes of trapped animals to describe the man who lacks *enkrateia*.[32] It would appear, therefore, that "rule" in Xenophon must not be always interpreted in an official sense but in a way which realizes that a ruler may be ruler of nothing more than himself and that he can be at the same time the servant of a king, a city, or a lord of the manor.

If the dialogue between Socrates and Aristippos teaches that the city is necessary by nature, it is not surprising that

Xenophon continues his investigation of this necessity by proceeding immediately to examine how the city is concerned in the relationships of a man with relatives and friends. It is evident that a man requires a mother for life itself and that he is naturally dependent upon her for nurture throughout his upbringing. Consequently hostility to a parent is a kind of ingratitude and the only one which the *polis* is eager to punish.[33] For, as Socrates tells his own son, if men see that someone is ungrateful to his parents, they cannot expect any gratitude from him should they themselves do him a kindness. A man deficient in his primary social relationship is a potential threat to the proper working of society in general, and society lets the punishment fit the crime by disqualifying him from office and letting him live destitute of friends, alone.[34] The same might be said concerning the relationship of brothers, for their harmony is a natural thing, as natural as a pair of hands and just as productive when they work together. The brother like the parent aids the individual in overcoming his inherent limitations.[35]

Friends, too, aid a man; and Xenophon stresses the similiarity between friend and kin by using of friends the same similes (hands and eyes) he had used in describing the mutual beneficence of brothers.[36] This naturalness of friendship is emphasized explicitly when Socrates answers the question of his young interlocutor Kritoboulos, "Who will be friends and in whom will trust and goodwill be found?" if even good men quarrel over preeminence:

> "Well, Kritoboulos," Socrates said, "these things are somewhat complicated. For human beings by nature possess dispositions to friendship; for they have need of one another and they feel compassion and, working together, they obtain advantage, and, being aware of this, they thank one another. They also have dispositions to enmity. . . . But nonetheless friendship, slipping through these, joins together the noble and the good."[37]

Friendship, it appears, is crucial to civic life, because it is a guarantee of continued harmony and a bulwark against internecine strife. Friends will not seek to outdo one another in getting honor, nor will they be inclined to seek power for their own solitary ends to the harm of everyone else.[38] This, of course, applies to men of virtue, the noble and the good; as in the conversation with Aristippos, the man who acts only in his own interest is not virtuous and is ultimately uncivic, and friends who conspire to do wrong cannot properly be considered true friends, since their own unscrupulousness and evil will inevitably drive them apart.[39] The true friend will not envy his comrade's prosperity and will consider his own possessions to be equally the other's. This community of interest and above all the disinclination to have more, *pleonexia*, are the hallmark of friendship and make it an essential part of life in the *polis*; for it is precisely in the desire to have more than is proper that warfare begins and injustice takes its start.[40]

The opening dialogues of the second book of the *Memorabilia* are concerned to establish the necessary dependence of the individual upon others and the need for a social life that begins with the family and culminates in the *polis*, which, fittingly enough, seeks to preserve those societal instincts which lead to its own existence.[41] The development from individual to *polis* is a natural phenomenon, so there cannot be any true opposition between the best interest of the city and the citizen, which is to say man, since man must be in the city. The conversation with Kritoboulos also suggests that the city is the commonwealth of family and friends and that, in its best state, it will know nothing of war. War, it is implied, is the enemy of polity, not war of defense naturally, but war of aggression. For the aggressor is the individual who asserts claims of his own over and above the city's, who does not recognize his own limitations. He attempts "to have more," and in so doing he must inevitably violate the natural rules of the city and thus become unjust. And in being unjust he is less a man.

The connection between proper civic life and justice, viewed as *nomos* opposed to *pleonexia*, becomes especially clear in the *Oikonomikos*. The noble and good man, Iskhomakhos, realizes his virtue by managing his household so it aims at advantage and sufficiency but not aggrandizement.

As Socrates once again in conversation with Kritoboulos reports his talk with Iskhomakhos, it becomes clear that the household is built upon an order in which everything is in its proper place, in readiness for its proper use. When Iskhomakhos educates his young wife to her duties, he asserts:

> For there is nothing, wife, as useful or as noble for men as order.[42]

This notion of order and arrangement rests upon the assumption that everything and everyone has a proper function which is, however, not universal in its applicability. Ordering is the act of someone recognizing the inherent capacities and limitations of a variety of persons or implements, so that by their grouping they may be used efficiently. Conversely disorder prevents anything useful being done and can even result in loss of life, if, for instance, a man is on a disordered ship foundering in a storm.[43]

If increase is possible only with an accurate appraisal of abilities and their proper organization, it is not surprising that the perfect enterprise for the man like Iskhomakhos is farming, the most basic science of growing things. Not surprising, either, is Socrates' perception that farming is the occupation most honored by the city because it exercises the bodies of those who practice it and makes them devoted to the land's protection from enemies; since farming is the most easy with its gifts, it gives men time to join in the affairs of friends and the city.[44] What is more the gods themselves concur with the actions of men. As Iskhomakhos tells his wife, nature brings forth things with differing capacities, and the law *(nomos)* praises this situation by joining, for instance, male and female in marriage:

> and just as god has made them sharers of children, so too the law establishes them as sharers of the house.[45]

The farmer, in planting the land as he does, first of all recognizes its nature and sows accordingly, "for it is no advantage to fight against the god."[46] In obtaining the proper kinds of household staff and farm overseers, the master must see to it that they do not take for themselves what is his, just as he himself, at least in Iskhomakos' case, must see to it that increase comes from noble and just action.[47] It is certainly with this imperative in mind that Iskhomakhos also tells Socrates that he has no use for stewards who are greedy (*pleonektas*) and that he considers as his equals those who strive for justice not just because they will obtain more (*pleon ekhein*) from him as a result of their virtue but because they desire his praise by itself.[48]

Iskhomakhos as a householder and a farmer is preeminently interested in securing order and justice; in other words his action is similar to that of the city's governor, who must also preserve law and order. This similarity causes Socrates to insist to Nikomakhides in the *Memorabilia* that rule of private things is not radically distinct from rule of public things:

> "Don't look down upon household managers, Nikomakhides," he said; "for the care for private affairs differs only in degree from that of public ones. In other aspects they are rather alike, most of all because neither sort can be done without human beings, nor are private matters handled by men of a different sort from those who handle the public."[49]

In agreement with this association of the individual and the public is Xenophon's consistent linking together of "having enough," justice, the city, and nature or the gods, and his opposing to them of "having more," injustice, the solitary life, and the violation of nature or despite of the gods. It would seem that, considered thus far, what is just and what is the city are easily reconcilable, that, indeed, the law of the city is what constitutes justice. In fact Socrates makes precisely this assertion to the notorious sophist Hippias of Elis.[50]

Xenophon further strengthens the union between the private and the public when in the third book of the *Memorabilia* he recounts a number of conversations between Socrates and men set on great occupations like generalship or on small ones like shield-making. Men must do the right thing and in the right way in view of their natural limitations. The very variety of Socrates' conversations in this section of the *Memorabilia* is witness to Xenophon's insistence on the need at all levels for a proper understanding of individual action and its purpose both for the individual and the city. Xenophon has deliberately arranged the structure of his work to highlight this emphasis. The third book, which begins with discussions about the relationship between a man and the larger units of an army or the city, ends with conversations progressively more concerned with people mastering those arts that affect individuals, until finally Xenophon concludes with Socrates' advice on the right control of the individual body in exercise and diet. Book Three is thus a mirror image of Book Two, which began with the particular (Aristippos and his self-control) and moved to the more general (son and mother, brother and brother, a man and his friends). The central section of the *Memorabilia* begins and ends with the individual and his concern to maintain himself properly, which means to fulfil himself as much as possible within the limitations of human nature as realized in the city. As Socrates tells Epigenes, being an *idiōtēs*, a resolutely private man, is not enough.[51] There is a sense in which a man may be unjust if he does too little. So Socrates can tell Kharmides, who is reluctant to enter into public affairs though clearly qualified to do so:

> "My good fellow, do not be ignorant of yourself, nor err in the way most err; for the majority, eager to look after the affairs of others, are not disposed to examine themselves."[52]

Knowledge of the self is thus the basis of justice, because it makes a man aware of his ability, which is to say, his limitation, and hence his inevitable need for others both as helpers in advancement and defenders in adversity. It therefore goes without saying that insofar as justice involves respect for others (and thus respect for oneself) and the city stands as the institution whereby this respect is best assured, what is *nomimon* (legal) and what is *dikaion* (just) are the same. Moreover since it is Socrates who expresses this view and since it is he who above all prompts all men to know themselves, he must be considered a just man, a man of the *polis*.

It would seem that Socrates is a pious man, because it is clear that he believes in the gods of the city, a belief which suits well his justice, since it is the gods who are the ultimate foundation of the city inasmuch as they have made the world as it is. One feature of this world, as Socrates points out to the "deist" Aristodemos, is its design, which reveals how many things accommodate to human benefit (the delicate eyes, for example, have lids and enable man to see what is visible) and intimate an intelligence responsible for their creation.[53] The gods, too, would seem to care for man, for they have given him more than other creatures, most notably the mind and the power of speech.[54] In another conversation, this time with his new student Euthydemos, with whom Socrates is interested in proceeding according to his own method of instruction, Socrates elaborates on the gifts of mind and language by stressing that it is through their agency that man is able to classify experience and devise means to win the good and avoid the harmful. Above all through speech man is able to share all good things with his fellows, to enact laws, and to live in organized cities (*politeuometha*).[55] Finally Socrates will win his point against Hippias of Elis when he says that the gods, in their unwritten laws, whose transgression will always bring a suitable punishment, have established that what is legal is also just.[56] The gods may be said to have set forth a model in their own actions and in their own enactments for men's imitation. Their primacy may also be inferred from the structure of the accusation against Socrates at his trial, for in Xenophon the first charge is that Socrates did not believe in the same gods as the city; and it is this question of Socrates' relation to the gods that Xenophon will always discuss first in the *Memorabilia* before describing his teacher's other virtues.[57]

It looks, therefore, as if the question "what is justice?" must ultimately become the question "what is god?" or "who are the gods?" Now in the *Memorabilia* this is a question Socrates does not raise, for all his talk about divinity. In his conversation with Aristodemos, moreover, he avoids answering directly one of Aristodemos' most penetrating complaints: do the gods care for the individual man?[58] An answer may, however, be found in the *Oikonomikos*, that work which so concerns itself with the natural basis of existence. There it is stated that a curious connection exists between the ordered and philanthropic activity of farming and the hostile activity of warfare. The land for farming is placed out in the open for the strongest to take,[59] and the gods are the gods of both war and peace.[60] The king of Persia takes as much interest in farming as in war,[61] and the farmer and the warlord may be considered kindred spirits:

> Frequently in war it is even safer to seek after sustenance with weapons than with farm tools. And farming also educates for the aiding of one another. For it is necessary to go with men against enemies, and working the earth requires men.[62]

The desire for increase, in other words, contains within itself by nature the potential of becoming a *Wille zur Macht*, just as men contain within themselves by nature a disposition to war as well as to friendship. As Socrates tells Kritoboulos:

> For men, when they think the same things noble and pleasant, fight for them, and when they disagree, oppose one another. Competition and anger are also warlike, and the passion for having more is hostile, while envy is hateful.[63]

In nature itself, therefore, as well as in man, a contradictory kind of action is possible. It would seem, that is to say, that the gods do not necessarily preserve those who live by order and within limitation. Socrates can in fact readily admit to Iskhomakhos that the gods do not rule the year in an ordered manner *(ou tetagmenōs)*,[64] while Iskhomakhos himself can report the testimony of a Phoenician sailor, who told him that order on a ship in storm, when everyone is doing just what he is supposed to, may not bring salvation:

> For the god threatens and punishes laggards. But if only he does not destroy those who do nothing amiss, a man must be very satisfied.[65]

Can the gods, therefore, destroy one who has done no wrong, can they be, as it were, unjust? Is there an opposition between what is structured and what is not, is there a conflict that cannot be surmounted between the city and nature? It may be that Xenophon's Socrates has perceived a certain truth in the opinion current amongst his contemporaries and judged subversive by many of them that *nomos* and *phusis*, law and nature, do not square. And if they do not, what is to become of justice both human and divine?

It thus becomes clear why Socrates does not answer with forthright assurance Aristodemos' question about the gods' philanthropy to the individual man, and also why he is so eager to prevent the young and hardly philosophic Kritoboulos from continuing with a question in the *Oikonomikos* whose full import Kritoboulos can not know and which, if he did know, might prove harmful.[66] For Kritoboulos begins to wonder whether it is possible in farming to foresee most things, especially given the occurence of storms, hail, blight, and disease. Socrates insists:

> "For know well," he said, "that those who are prudent, for the sake of fruits and grains and cattle and horses and sheep and all they possess honor the gods."[67]

But in spite of Socrates' anxiety to preserve amongst his associates a proper reverence and honor for the gods, there still remains the suspicion that Socrates may not have been just and pious as the city conventionally defined those terms. His knowledge could be dangerous.

The city may have had other reasons for being suspicious about Socrates as well. If farming is the occupation it sets most store by, and if it honors those who manage their households well, like Iskhomakhos, Socrates must certainly have appeared less than the best citizen. Xenophon in the *Oikonomikos* makes it clear, in fact, that Iskhomakhos and Socrates represent two different approaches to life.[68] To say the least the noble and good farmer is not a man of thought, and Socrates must at times almost catch his breath in astonishment as his friendly partner in conversation blithely recounts to him how he teaches justice or how firm and unshakeable is his belief in total order.[69] He also wonders at Iskhomakhos' great concern for money and the increase of money; but Iskhomakhos explains by saying that without money he could not honor the gods in a splendid way or help his friends or keep the city adorned.[70] Socrates, of course, was a monetarily poor man, he hardly handled his wife as well as Iskhomakhos, and he could do nothing lavish. In fact he had the reputation of being an idler.[71]

But Socrates is aware that he is nonetheless a good man; and he has learned this, as only Xenophon's Socrates could, from a horse, a champion thoroughbred, who, though owning nothing, is still the object of everyone's attention because he is good by nature.[72] Socrates, in other words, abstracts from his experience with the horse something which applies to him, even though he and the horse are hardly alike in all respects. Socrates has made an analogy, and not for nothing does he exclaim in his conversation with Iskhomakhos how that gentleman makes a greater impression on him by using likenesses than by simply droning on about one detail after another.[73] Iskhomakhos himself will become a likeness for Kritoboulos when Socrates discusses with his young companion what is the noble and good man and what constitutes that kind of life. But what is most important is how this use of analogy implies that there is a certain sameness in things as well as difference. Therefore to say that Socrates is not Iskhomakhos, that he is not, in other words, alleged to be the best citizen, does not mean that Socrates in his life of the mind is not really a citizen or that he transcends the city. He is not, of course, the economist Iskhomakhos is, but it is from Iskhomakhos that Socrates takes instruction. His life and thought are thus rooted in the *polis,* and what Socrates subsequently thinks and teaches does not have to be seen as an indication of his ineluctable opposition to the city. It does not reveal a kind of Machiavellian tension between the requirements of the just life and the city's life but rather a continuing effort to make the city what it best ought to be. Socrates as a great teacher invites the city to a higher vision of itself, just as he invited the foppish and disdainful Kallias in the *Symposium* to live up to his nature and the requirement of his family's civic traditions.

There may be a very real way, that is to say, in which Socrates is an economist and even a ruler. For Socrates and Kritoboulos both agree that the economist is the man who uses what he has to good advantage and increase.[74] Now Socrates is a man who clearly possesses next to nothing, and yet he can jokingly claim that he is far richer than the very wealthy Kritoboulos.[75] The joke is not a lie, for Socrates does possess at least his friends, and it is these in conjunction with his mental capacity that he uses to advantage and increase more than any other man. In so doing he lives a life of sufficiency, *autarkeia*, which does not require him to amass monetary wealth or to yearn for more than he needs. By definition, therefore, his life has the least potential for being unjust.

But it can be objected that if Socrates is, as it were, his own master, his life has about it an inevitably solitary or uncivic aspect which does not permit him to engage in what the city thinks is most important. Xenophon attempts to counter this charge by insisting throughout his Socratic works that Socrates was through and through a man of the city. Socrates, of course, was always before everyone's eyes in the public places and could be said to be more civic in this sense than even Iskhomakhos, who spent most of his time on his farm.[76] Furthermore as conversation after conversation in the *Memorabilia* shows, he attempts constantly to make people such as Kritoboulos, or the son of Perikles, or Aristippos, or Aristodemos just the kind of men the city so admired. And of course he also seeks to benefit the city by seeking to insure the mutual concord of its members.

But does Socrates have what might be called a "secret life"? Does his life ultimately ignore or conflict with public concern?[77] When Xenophon describes the association of Socrates and his closest friends, he intimates nothing about the uncivic nature of their activity. He contrasts, in fact, their true concern for benefiting the city and their fellow-citizens with the actions of men like Alkibiades who seek their own honor and glory, their *philotimia*, through politics, which to them means demagoguery and courtroom wrangling.[78] Xenophon thus opposes the action of Socrates and his best friends not with the political life of the city but with its corruption. In the same way as well, he reports the interesting conversation Socrates has with the sophist Antiphon, who wants Socrates' students for his own. Antiphon attacks the philosopher for his poor life without money and says he is a teacher of misery and of nothing useful; he voices precisely those objections which good and proper citizens might have voiced.[79] But Socrates can in reply show

how he is hardly miserable, since he is in fact most free; and if he is free, and not a slave to comfort and luxury, he is most truly the man of the free *polis*, who can respond more readily than others to its call and who can undergo hardship for its sake more easily. Furthermore selling wisdom for money is rather like the disreputable business of the prostitute whereas Socrates, who teaches for nothing, is acting like the good and reputable citizen.[80] What Socrates does is to share with his friends whatever good he can impart, and they derive from their friendship a mutually beneficial understanding of the wise men of old, which constitutes a true treasure and gain.[81]

But Antiphon is apparently not yet satisfied. Talking with friends is not necessarily an activity of the good citizen, since men can conspire to overthrow the city. How, then, he asks Socrates, can Socrates make men "political," if he himself does not do "the political things?" Socrates replies:

> "Antiphon," he said, "would I be doing the political things more if I should do them by myself or if I should take care that as many as possible are capable of doing them?"[82]

This is an important response, because it suggests not only how Socrates differs from the sophists but also because it points the way to solving the problem of the relationship between Socrates and the city and Socrates and justice. To be political does not mean to be an active seeker of glory — to be addicted to *philotimia* — or to be the financial and civic bulwark Iskhomakhos is. It may be that Socrates sees in this a danger which is all too apparent in men like Alkibiades or Kritias and in teachers like Antiphon. For his reply indicates that being political is not doing something alone and for personal glory but by necessity doing something with others for everyone's advantage. Antiphon's criticism of Socrates' life thus turns out to reveal by implication the essential flaw of his own sophistic life. For it is a life based not so much upon wealth and comfort as upon a sense of personal supremacy by which all actions are gauged and all goals sought. Antiphon as a sophist really has no need for other men save as paying audiences; he can talk without addressing anyone.

Socrates, on the contrary, requires another person in order to do what he does; to engage in conversation without an interlocutor or a respondent is a contradiction in terms.[83] Insofar as he recognizes this need for someone beyond himself as it affects him in his most essential activity, he can be said to have a more complete appreciation than other men of the basic need which culminates in civic life. Socrates is just, then, not only because he tries to make as many as possible fit citizens in whatever activity is theirs but because he knows more fully than most that precisely because of his nature as a man he can never live alone. To disregard the city would be to deny his existence; to deny his existence by insisting on solitude would be unjust because he would then be seeking to have too much, to be more than was human.

Socrates tells Antiphon that he is most blest when reading together with his companions the classic books. In the *Oikonomikos* it is said that a man can not be blest without being "economic."[84] Once again, therefore, Socrates' manner of life reveals its civic nature. Far from being an idler and a wastrel, Socrates constantly works to learn more and to benefit his friends and the city by what he knows. For knowledge of the self to which he invites his companions is not an invitation to self-aggrandizement but to the fulfillment of the self that could only come from a recognition of the limits of the self. It is no wonder, then, that Socrates' essential activity brings him into necessary contact with others, for only in his friends can he fully achieve his aim. He is, that is to say, the quintessentially friendly man, who sees love spring not from the superficial attractions of the body but from the profound requirements of human nature. His whole life may be said to look forward to a society of friends who would know no enemies. And in this society Socrates will not only be a citizen but its very ruler, and the best sort of ruler, because he is able to obtain in his conversations anything he wants by persuasion and not by force.[85] Finally if the city is the polity of men living in concord and not in mutual hostility, and abiding by justice and not by might, Socrates may lay claim to being the most perfect citizen. Xenophon is thus not all that reckless in proposing, in the last book of the *Memorabilia*, as his ultimate defense of Socrates the Socratic method itself.[86] As he says in its opening pages, the intimates of Socrates are those whom the philosopher knows to be good natures from their desire to learn to benefit not only themselves but other men and cities,[87] while in conversation with a new student, Euthydemos, Xenophon's Socrates points out that self-knowledge must lead to a sense of needs for the self which cannot be met by the individual alone.[88]

The *polis*, therefore, has little cause to suspect Socrates either as a public or a private man; and it is worth noting that in Xenophon Socrates is never discovered in the solitary trances Plato occasionally describes, just as in Xenophon the structure of political life seems to derive more from a consideration of the relations of men with one another than from the contemplation of the structure of the individual's soul. Even Socrates' knowledge that the gods do not always respect the ordered structure men or cities place upon nature does not have to lead to doubt about the claims of order or the city. For to say that *nomos* is not *phusis* is an overstatement. Rather Xenophon suggests that *nomos* is the *phusis* of man, though man is not the whole of nature, and so neither is *nomos*. But since *nomos* does derive from the world as the gods made it, it may be considered as the justice required for human life and sanctioned by divinity. This is not of course a very flattering notion for those who proclaim that man is the measure of all things, but as Xenophon observes of Socrates immediately after his conversation with Antiphon, Socrates is not an *alazōn*,[89] an imposter who makes himself out to be bigger than he is. So too Socrates can teach that there are some things the gods do not want man to know[90] and that he himself, by freeing himself from the compulsions of the passions and overindulgence, is most free and most close to the gods; yet he is never divine but only the most perfectly human of men.[91]

Xenophon's Socrates never achieves that exaltation found by Plato in the contemplation of the eternal and immutable Forms, and he suggests that human life cannot ever be absolutely sure of anything. So Socrates prays to the gods for whatever they think is good, since to pray for gold or silver or unlimited power *(tyrannida)* is no different from praying for a throw of the dice or a battle or anything risky.[92] It seems that in the end the Xenophon who can speak in more than mere metaphor when he calls the good ruler a father, because in one sense the *polis* is a natural outgrowth of the family, may see more in analogy than a means of instruction or a witness to an internal consistency of nature on its various levels. Socrates' use of analogy, that is, may derive from the more penetrating perception that men cannot expect to live with abiding certitude that anything will always be what it seems to them; they must, rather, live "as if." This perhaps explains why Xenophon says Socrates considers it sophistic folly to talk of the cosmos[93] and why he never claims to be a teacher of virtue. He is instead a likeness for his companions to imitate, and he makes those who follow his example have the hope—but not the certainty—that they will become noble and good men *(kalous kagathous).*[94]

It remains a fact, however, that Socrates was condemned. The uncertainty of life proved itself in his case with a vengeance; for how could the most just of men be found unjust? As Xenophon shows in the *Apology,* Socrates maintains that he has lived a pious and just life and that his life was his defense.[95] But Socrates' life is the life of friendship, and he is never interested in harming his enemies. At most he overcomes them in speech; but he can not compel anyone's obedience to the truth he represents. His power, no less than the power of any man, is finally limited; and it can not overcome the folly of his judges.[96] This is doubtless one explanation for his reluctance to make any speech of defense during his trial, a resolve which the observation of Hermogenes does little to weaken. Does not Socrates realize, he says,

> in the courts of the Athenians frequently they execute those who are innocent, being induced by a speech, and frequently they acquit those guilty, out of pity for what they have said or because they have spoken pleasingly?[97]

Yet Socrates finally does speak; and when he does, he

does so extravagantly. He talks big, and it is this big talk which is Xenophon's particular interest in his smallest Socratic work.[98] If Socrates' actions are in agreement with his words, the explanation of his peculiar address to the jury, which only inflames them against him, may be found in the nature of his life. If his actions have been a striving towards perfection, it will only be fitting that his words stress that claim to perfection. Furthermore if words, especially in an Athenian court, are often lies, it really does not matter ultimately what he says, since the proper use of speech is meaningless there. But even more important, if everyone else in court says, as it were, too little in order to justify himself, Socrates with his mordant sense of humor will say too much and thus throw into glaring relief the difference between his life and the life of his accusers. He will tell the *whole* truth, he will say that he is more pious and true in speaking of his special *daimōn*, that he is special because that *daimōn* never advises him wrongly both in telling him what to do and what not to do, that he has been engaged in the best occupation, and that he is its best practitioner.[99] Socrates in the *Apology* does not compromise, for to do so would be to pervert the meaning of his life and to make him little better than the perverters of justice who attack him. Socrates in fact outsmarts them at their own wretched game, for by serving up to them just what they hate, he manages to show up their impiety and their injustice. Another Xenophontic figure only talks big prior to engaging his enemies;[100] Socrates' foes stand forth as the subverters of the city from within.

It is the god, moreover, who tells Socrates that he should prefer death to life.[101] His piety thus reaches its climax in his acceding to that demand, even as his justice is vindicated by the god's implication that Socrates has no need to go to court. In view of this Socrates will not permit his friends to pay a fine for him, since it would be tantamount to an admission of guilt, and when they suggest spiriting him away, he asks them whether death does not go elsewhere than Attika.[102] Socrates' equanimity before death, rendered all the more impressive by the lack of any uplifting talk about going to a better place,[103] represents the final expression of his humanity in the face of the ineluctable human experience and the sealing of human limit. But there also remains an awareness that Socrates is meant to die by the very nature of his life not as a man but precisely as the best man. From the time he was born, he tells his weeping companions, he was under sentence of death; from the time he knew what was said to him, he tells his judges, he never ceased searching out and learning whatever he could.[104] Socrates dies because he has lived his life with an earnestness which most men find excessive and irritating. But Xenophon suggests that their irritation is more at their own inability to live as perfectly as Socrates, for he says that Socrates' judges hate him out of envy.[105] They begrudge him his life because it is more valuable than their own, but even in their spite they establish his virtue as a citizen. For envy, as Xenophon defines it, is dismay and sorrow at the success of friends.[106] Socrates' death affirms his love of the city; and he prefers to die being just rather than to live by an injustice.[107]

Philosophy, it has been said, begins with astonishment, the sense of wondering how something could be so. Xenophon begins the *Memorabilia*, his remembrances of Socrates, by mentioning that he has often wondered how the Athenians could have convicted his teacher. This is not, as Kierkegaard would have it,[108] the dull surprise of someone who can see in Socrates only a boring burgher, but the startling and disturbing awareness that all attempts at a lasting perfection seem inevitably undone and that the excellent man is thrown back upon himself as much in sorrow as in vindication. Xenophon's philosophy arises from his interest in an individual man and the relation of that man to the *polis*. It is a peculiarly human philosophy which in its concern with Socrates inevitably leads Xenophon to consider in everything he wrote the meaning of the philosopher's first maxim, which was also the maxim of the god at Delphi: know thyself. It does not concern itself with the search for transcending certitude and absolutes through metaphysical inquiry, not because Xenophon did not have a capable intellect, but because he probably did not believe in the nature or the object of such a quest. Xenophon's is a philosophy which refuses to indulge the desire for the beyond, and he does not speak of this "beyond," if only because he surely felt that, even if it was real, it was ineffable. If Xenophon's understanding of Socrates did not lead him to the Forms, neither did it lose him in the clouds. Ultimately he remains in *aporia*.

3

CYRUS

*Les plus grands sujets doivent toujours aller
au delà du vraisemblable.* —Corneille

Persia always fascinated the Greeks. Herodotos and Aeschylus must have had as eager audiences in the fifth century as Ktesias had in the fourth. Cyrus the Great seems to have attracted special interest, and legends about him quickly gathered in places as diverse as Greece and Judaea. Amongst the Socratics Antisthenes wrote two dialogues named after him, and he also became the protagonist of the *Kyroupaideia,* Xenophon's most extended work. Xenophon's choice of subject need not, therefore, be taken as an indication of some new cosmopolitanism, nor a reflection of his own travels abroad, especially since the Persian ingredient in the *Kyroupaideia* is little more than a flavoring. More likely he was prompted by the opportunity a legendary figure provided for presenting an ideal of action on the largest scale possible. Xenophon wished to discuss how government succeeded, in view of the fact that in his own age none seemed to;[1] and Cyrus, having become a figure of myth, was a happy convenience, since he ruled successfully the largest kingdom known to Xenophon's time. The ideal and the historical could merge to create the first novel, a mimesis in prose. History turned to fiction could permit the elucidation of ideas concerning the typical and the timeless.

Comparisons with the actual history of Cyrus as Herodotos preserves it[2] illuminate Xenophon's method and point. The real Cyrus was a rebel whose grandfather wanted him exposed at birth; the Cyrus of Xenophon has a happy childhood with his parents—he was decidedly not raised by a cowherd—and his mother's father Astyages cannot help but dote on him like any good grandpapa. Xenophon has made right what actually went wrong; the family of his future hero is sound and harmonious, and Cyrus' greatest teacher, as the extended dialogue at the end of the first book is meant to show, was none other than his father Kambyses. In the same spirit the system of education Xenophon describes does not allow the younger boys a communal barracks life; they continue to live with their parents until they become ephebes at age sixteen or seventeen, and only then do they spend the night away from home. Even amongst this latter group, those who marry can receive dispensations.[3] The family, it appears, is crucial to Xenophon's conception of an ordered society. This emphasis remains throughout the Kyroupaideia and can been seen, for example, in Cyrus' careful regard for his lacklustre uncle, Kyaxares, and his continuing respect, great king though he had become, for his own parents, not to mention his concern for his own children.[4] The family, it is clear, provides the individual with his first social sense and is the nursery for the hero's later excellence.

If the family by definition helps to broaden the individual's awareness, Xenophon seeks to extend that awareness by his "Persian" paideia, whose openness is its hallmark. Instruction is carried on away from the hurly-burly of the business place in the "free market"[5] and is concerned specifically with justice, the standard by which relations with others are directed. It is clear that this justice involves respect for the property of others, since theft is condemned outright, and that justice must use persuasion, not force, when seeking to improve an unfortunate situation.[6] It is fitting that the greatest wrong should be thanklessness:

> And whoever they know is capable of returning thanks but does not do it they punish severely. For they think that the thankless would be most careless of the gods and their parents and their fatherland and their friends.[7]

There is something particularly human in gratitude; and Xenophon has the commoner Pheraulas realize this, who avers, using as a corroborative example the regard humans have for parents, that man stands apart from the animals because he is more gracious and responds more positively to kindness than beasts do.[8]

The Persian *paideia* extends throughout several stages encompassing a human lifetime, and promotion in grade is consequent upon success in the one immediately preceding.[9] What is curious about Cyrus, however, is that he does not pursue this program without interruption, for he spends a goodly time away from Persia visiting his grandfather in Media. His mother is aware of a possible danger, for her father has had little to do with the inculcation of justice:

> So don't be undone if you are whipped whenever you are at home, if you come from grandfather's having learned not kingliness but tyranny, in which it is usual to think it necessary to have the most of everything.[10]

The young Cyrus, with his usual charm, assures his mother that she has nothing to fear; but his own actions in Media betray in him a spirit not totally in harmony with the life back home. He is something of a bully to the hapless senechal Sakas, he actively seeks out the dangerous in hunts when specifically told not to, and, in an important battle encounter, he acts without forethought, like a well-bred but inexperienced hound going after a boar.[11] Cyrus' spirit is enterprising and unafraid of the novel. As a child he seems to have something which sets him apart and allows him a freedom it is to be imagined few of his fellows in Persia can safely enjoy. He is special by nature, not only by training or education; and although he will return to Persia and fulfil the demands of its *paideia*, he seeks, when leading an army for the first time, to invite his troops to a new conception of the Persian way of doing things. He tells them that their ancestors had too quiet and passive a sense of justice and virtue which gained nothing for themselves or their commonwealth. Cyrus appeals for a more active understanding and says that virtue should bring rewards, honor, and glory. Otherwise it would rather resemble the case of the farmer who plants and husbands his land well but deliberately lets the harvest die on the ground, uncollected.[12] This new, active spirit with which Cyrus attempts to infuse the old Persian system is a significant change and opens up the

Persian horizon to include the world. And so it is that Cyrus' typical activity in the Kyroupaideia is the winning of new territory and glory for himself and his allies.

But Cyrus' winning of more and seeking for advantage does not violate justice. He neither seeks out, nor initiates any of his wars, and he begins his career of campaigning only after an invitation from the Medes, who have been first wronged by others.[13] Cyrus does not indulge in pleonexia; and when he finally returns home to Persia, his father warns him against its dangers and points out the necessity of mutual assistance between a ruler and citizens, if a happy polity is to be maintained.[14] Cyrus appreciates this lesson; and he is concerned that his own children and those of his friends receive an understanding of justice,[15] just as he knows it was folly to boast and act lordly before his self-pitying uncle, after he had made conquests which put Kyaxares to shame.[16] For all his sense of personal resolve and ability, Cyrus recognizes a limit to his power and the necessity, if he is to preserve it, to utilize and respect the services of others. Yet it is typical that, even as he always rewards those who aid him, he esteems someone like Khrysantas more than Hystaspas; for although Hystaspas did all he was commanded to, Khrysantas did not wait to be commanded but acted on his own initiative when he knew something better could be done for all.[17] Cyrus may have remembered an incident from his youth in Media, when he learned that a man's sense of duty should derive from his own self-awareness and not from the rebukes or exhortations of others. After he had tantalized his young friends with the desire to go on a real hunt outside the safety of Astyages' paradise garden, his eager companions told him they could share his exhilaration only if he secured his grandfather's approval. In the face of his reluctance to entreat on their behalf, they called it scandalous that they should have to seek from another what they ought to expect from him. And when he heard this Cyrus was stung.[18]

It is above all this sense of enterprise and respect for justice, which gives the lie to those who see in the Kyroupaideia a historical allegory, who transform Cyrus and the Persians into Agesilaos and the Spartans, while insisting that the Assyrians equal contemporary Persians who are to be the object of one of Isokrates' holy wars.[19] This is too simple. The system of *paideia* Xenophon describes has little in common with the Spartan. It is ostensibly open to all, not just to one class,[20] military training is neither its sole nor main object, and such famous Spartan lessons as those in theft are inimical to its spirit. Its openness is utterly foreign to the Spartan temperament, and Spartans, unlike Cyrus, were notoriously bad travellers. And when Spartans do figure in the text, the references are hardly flattering; on one occasion they are the sought-after ally of Croesus, not of Cyrus, while on another Xenophon compares the Assyrians' high-handed treatment of the Hyrcanians to Sparta's treatment of the Skiritai.[21] It is, in any event, inconceivable that Xenophon, writing the *Kyroupaideia* probably around 362, could have considered the loser at Leuktra and the helpless victim of Epameinondas' incursions into the Peloponnesos as the leader of Greece.[22] It would have been the act not of an idealist but of a fool.

There are any number of ways in which the activity of Cyrus differs from the regimen of Sparta. Cyrus is enterprising because he knows next to nothing of fear. Fear is something he has to learn about from others, and he receives his best instruction from the Armenian prince Tigranes. Tigranes and Cyrus have been boyhood friends, but the former's father has revolted from the Medes, and Cyrus is called in to aid his own relatives in suppression of the Armenian rebel. Naturally Cyrus vanquishes Tigranes' father, leaving his old friend the task of pleading for his parent's life. Tigranes' shrewd arguments are amazing and must be attributed to his schooling by a wise man, whom the king executed for allegedly corrupting his son.[23] Tigranes tells his conqueror that prudence, *sophrosunē*, derives from knowledge, but that fear enslaves. Fear paralyzes action and ends in death:

> For some, fearing lest they die if caught, die from fear beforehand, some hurling themselves off precipices, others hanging themselves, still others slashing their throats. Thus of all dread things fear most especially overwhelms spirits.[24]

Fear is general and results from ignorance; it does not discern. The Armenian is as abased in fear as Cyrus is exalted in his confidence. Confidence does not dwell in the shadows; Cyrus means his men to display their ability, and he is thankful to any who give him the chance of making manifest what sort of man he himself is.[25] Thus he can tell Tigranes' father to keep his wealth and finery, since it is sufficient to keep the body hidden and unadorned when each man lies buried in death.[26] Cyrus' army goes forth with its bronze armor gleaming like gold. His own is like a mirror, and his tent faces the dawn.[27]

The companion of confidence is the laughter which slays fright. Cyrus tells some of his troops that because of their expertise they will see, even before fighting, what jokes (geloious) the enemy are.[28] Naturally enough Cyrus and his men continually exchange humorous remarks and frequently enjoy jolly symposia. Even the grouch Aglaitadas is compelled to smile when Hystaspas says that it would be easier to extract fire from him than a laugh.[29] Aglaitadas has just proposed the theory that prudence is instilled more by tears than by kindness:

> "And justly, by Zeus," Aglaitadas said, "for it seems to me that the man who contrives laughter for his friends accomplishes for the most part less worthwhile things than the man who gets them used to crying."[30]

Aglaitadas would doubtless have found a warm welcome amongst the Lacedaemonians where beating was integral to the educational system, but Cyrus does not agree with him. As he told his uncle Kyaxares, a man encourages another to do what is good more by pleasing him than by grieving or forcing him.[31] Needless to say Cyrus does not mean to encourage unbridled malice or sarcasm, and he makes clear to Aglaitadas that humor is not synonymous with bragging; friends and companions do not joke for their own gain or for any harmful reason, but are more properly called urbane and charming (asteioi . . . kai eukharites) than braggarts (alazones).[32] Cyrus' sense of humor thus seems to be a part of his sense of society, a society not founded on doubt, fear, and mistrust, but on confident self-awareness which trusts that freedom will not be an inducement to self-aggrandizement.[33] Tears are for enemies,[34] and fear, as Tigranes knows, is a compulsion. "Sport is the bloom and glow of a perfect health."[35]

Hilarity, however, is not bred of indolence. Discipline and constant exercise alone will bring the steadfastness and knowledge which permit laughter even at personal expense. Cyrus is no blind enthusiast, and as a mature leader he seems to have overcome the unthinking passion of his youth. In fact he has what is no less than a passion for the ordered and the specific. He is concerned, as general, with one thing, waging the war, and his soldiers are to turn their attention to this and this only, for he has learned, Xenophon says, that those are best who turn their minds from many things to the one work at issue.[36] He sees to it that every soldier prepares himself to be as fit as possible; and he arranges various hunts and contests to develop their proper virtues, since the hunt is a playful image of the work of war.[37] His regard for the exercise of every individual enables him safely to exhort his army with a call not to general action but to each soldier's personal involvement in the fighting.[38]

The army is a large mass, but its organization is articulated, not amorphous; it is carefully divided into taxiarchies, pemparchies, decarchies, chiliarchies, and so on, up to the commander-in-chief. These groups are assigned specific tasks so that they may learn their function in the general group: they are to be at the right place at the right time with their needed contribution to the successful working of the whole. The commanders of the smaller groups must, by their individual actions, serve as models for their subordinates. Neither they nor their men are to be aloof from one another; the two must work together if victory is the goal.[39] Cyrus makes a point of knowing his subordinates by name, just as a doctor, he thinks, has to know the names of the individual organs and drugs with which he deals. If neither doctor nor commander has exact knowledge, nothing will get done, and even death may result.[40] Cyrus is also accessible to his men and often invites separate battalions as well as individual soldiers to dine with him.[41] Although

Pheraulas has made sure that Cyrus will reward everyone according to his merits and not make indiscriminate allocations of booty and prizes, personal merit is rendered more feasible when each contingent functions together. The structure of Cyrus' command strives to preserve a beneficial tension between the individual and the group, so that each reinforces the other to their mutual advantage.

Thus the group does not submerge its members; though they dine together and carry the same weaponry, the men do not become faceless. Individual differences are preserved because they are essential. Cyrus' own special excellence lies behind the realization that no two men are alike in daring; and daring, whetted, wins battles.[42] Self-confidence grows from interaction with others bent on displaying a fitting excellence, and trust in them discourages cowardice. As Cyrus understands it, mutual knowledge increases a personal sense of shame, whereas those unacquainted with each other can more easily backslide, as though they live in darkness.[43] Confidence which results from hard work and constant training with others is the basis of order. Order is sure and liberating. When plunged into any battle, Cyrus' men can overcome its confusion. Using one of his favorite images, Xenophon concludes the third book of the Kyroupaideia with a disciplined calm which transcends the pell-mell of the preceding scene of conflict:

> When they were out of the range of the missiles, they stood in place, knowing much more accurately than a chorus where each of them ought to be.[44]

Precision brings safety in time of war.

In his expansive drive both as general and later as king, Cyrus never loses sight of the particular. While in the field he shows an inventive interest in details of weapons and uniform. He develops a new type of chariot and even experiments with camel warfare.[45] Horses, too (as might be expected), merit a good deal of attention, with individual types singled out and kinds of armor appropriate for the parts of their bodies differentiated.[46] By the same token in the multiplicity of his realm at peace he recognizes the opportunity for the greatest possible excellence, for a greater division of labor, its particularlizing, will beget better quality.⁴⁷ But just as in the military sphere private action can not of itself bring victory, so in the political, trust in others is the only bulwark against discord and instability. Thus Xenophon reports how Khrysantas, with his typical common sense, once remarked that men are more easily beaten in battles the moment they individually seek their own safety, while Cyrus reminds his sons that the preserver of a kingdom is not an outward trapping of authority, like the sceptre, but the king's most trusted friends.⁴⁸

Against such a will and understanding Cyrus' enemies stand little chance. They are without order and without training; one leader must practically threaten his troops to go forth.⁴⁹ But as Cyrus assures Khrysantas, who worries lest the enemy's words of exhortation enable his army to be valorous, speech can no sooner make someone brave than a song well sung can make a musician out of someone who has not learned solfege.⁵⁰ Words, as Xenophon frequently points out, have a limited capacity, and speech can hold little sway over developed might. If they recall their past training and past victories, Cyrus' men can stand fortified against an attacking army. For their real enemy is not that army but their fear of it. It is the general unknown they go against, their greatest opponent is simply "the Assyrian." Xenophon gives him, that is, no specific name in a work otherwise replete with them.

A man only too happy to be beaten by Cyrus is the Lydian king Croesus. Croesus has come to understand that he has lost because he overestimated himself, especially when it comes to fighting against a man, descended from the gods and a line of kings, who practices virtue from childhood. Croesus is filled with euphoria as he contemplates enjoying in the future the most blessed form of life. This, he believes, is the life led by his wife:

> For she shared equally with me all the good things and all the soft things and all the pleasant things, but as for the anxieties of war and battle which make these things possible she shared not a whit.⁵¹

Croesus rejects the life of effort which alone, as Cyrus sees it, brings renown and insures freedom. Xenophon never says that Cyrus admired Croesus' wisdom, if wisdom it is; and it may well be wondered whether in boasting of his self-knowledge Croesus only betrays his penetrating folly. Cyrus, it will be appreciated, can hardly begin to understand his captive's attitude; and he merely displays amazement at the Lydian's easy temper, keeping him in his retinue because he may prove useful and because it may be safer than to let him go free.[52] Cyrus, it seems, regards Croesus' protestations with suspicion; he can not believe a man really means such things.

In contrast is the genuine concern Cyrus shows for the woman Pantheia; and it is surely as a correction of Croesus' lacklustre quietism that Xenophon chooses to recount her heroic and moving death immediately after Croesus' praise of womanish ease. Pantheia constantly proves her strength of character by resisting illicit amorous advances and by sharing so completely in the most difficult troubles of her husband Abradatas. Abradatas, inspired by her, prays that he may be worthy of her,[53] and upon his death in battle Pantheia slays herself and wins the high regard of the great Cyrus.[54] The vignettes of Abradatas and Pantheia begin a tradition in the Greek novel, but Pantheia's true heirs are not the silly damsels of a decadent genre. Her kin are women like Shakespeare's Cleopatra who have immortal longings in them.

Thus considered, these scenes are not a relief from the action of the *Kyroupaideia* but a heightening of it; for the *Kyroupaideia*, if anything, is a prose epic in which Cyrus becomes the new paradigm of heroic action. Clearly the best man, who won by his own initiative a vast empire, he even conquers Egypt; and he acquires Media by marrying its princess, as Xenophon once again changes history to increase the scope of his champion's accomplishments.[55] Unlike Kyaxares, Cyrus does not equate kingship with the license to be regal. He does not care for dissipation but wants to provide the motivating and controlling spirit for everything. He is at once the nonpareil and the model for his subordinates. Croesus sees in him a man descended not only from kings but from gods; Artaozos, the Mede who wants Cyrus' love, recruits his countrymen for Cyrus' campaigns by saying that he himself will never leave the side of a man so noble, excellent, and god-descended.[56] One scholar was reminded of Homer when he read the *Kyroupaideia*, though he was reluctant to admit it.[57] To be sure, Cyrus, the creation of a fourth-century philosopher, is not as emotionally compelling as Achilles or Odysseus; but his norm of action is as mastering as theirs, his commitment to it no less tenacious, and his achievements no less grand. The epic stance of the *Kyroupaideia* is clear and becomes all the more so with the realization that the very form of the novel had its roots in the epic; it transfers to prose, in an age when prose had become the dominant medium of serious thought, the liberties and values of the older poetic genre.[58]

The entire life of Cyrus represents an ideal of action. Criticism that *Kyroupaideia* is a misleading title, since only its first book concerns Cyrus' education, thus misses Xenophon's point, namely, that a proper *paideia* is an on-going process in which certain things are learned and done at certain times in accordance with the ability of an increasing maturity. It is decidedly not mere instruction for the young, if only because Xenophon sees no point at which a man can say he is finished with learning. Did not the old Socrates continually affirm his ignorance? Furthermore, Xenophon's emphasis, especially in the *Kyroupaideia*, on the necessity to act and to act constantly, avoiding the self-satisfied and soft contentment of a Croesus, is complemented by his notion that *paideia* encompasses all the ages of man. And insofar as Cyrus embodies and enacts this, he becomes the subject of the "education of Cyrus" as well as its object, since Xenophon presents him as a model for imitation. Xenophon's vision reveals once again his continuing regard for the particular (here the different stages of life with their different capacities) within a general context (here the human lifetime).[59]

In fact Cyrus' greatest glory can be said to come at the end of his campaigning, when he finally has to learn to govern a kingdom and, eventually, a vast empire at peace.

As he comes to realize, becoming a good man is no guarantee that one will remain so, unless care is taken through to the end.[60] Responsibility is even greater after success, since there is always the danger of succumbing to present pleasure. Cyrus' task is imposing, and he must have appreciated more than he had as a youth the words of his father that the man is doing something wondrous *(thaumaston)*[61] who so rules over people that they have what they need for life and become the kind of people they ought to be. Indeed rule can be a burden, especially when business means less leisure for friends' company, or the necessity to encumber oneself with elaborate trappings and regalia, or becoming royally remote when rule extends over hostile nations.[62] The king has to observe the written laws, for he is not a law unto himself; but he also has to be, as a good ruler, a "seeing law" *(bleponta nomon)* for men, since written justice can not always observe and punish a disrupter of order.[63] Cyrus' rule thus shows him once again securing what he thinks best for himself, namely, honor and glory, by adherence to societal norms and a personal regard for those beneath him. His role of commander and king can thus be likened to the action of a good father, as Khrysantas is quick to remark:

> for fathers look out for their children that good things will never fail them, while Cyrus now seems to me to be advising us how we may best carry on our lives in prosperity.[64]

The ideal of action presented in the *Kyroupaideia* is clearly akin to views about the life of the city which Xenophon takes in his Socratic works. That Cyrus is an imperial monarch and not the democratic or oligarchic governor of a city need not be taken to imply that Xenophon meant to propose monarchy as the best form of government, for Cyrus' kingship is a metaphor of an intellectual and artistic ideal. Cyrus is a king, as it were, because heroes are kings and not archons. Yet the striking feature of the *Kyroupaideia*, considering its philosopher-author, is the absence of philosophy and philosophers within its pages. It would be prosaic in the extreme to suggest that Socrates (or a surrogate) is not present in the *Kyroupaideia*, because even its fancy can not violate history so, but it is also going too far in the other direction to suggest that Socrates' absence betokens Xenophon's perception that the life of the philosopher ultimately lies beyond the life of the city or that there exists some latent hostility between the two.[65]

Xenophon's Socrates and Cyrus have too much in common to warrant a radical segregation. Both possess a similar self-control, both honor the gods, both are rulers of themselves. Both have an analogous task: to dispose men to care about the right things in the right way. Thus Xenophon can describe Cyrus' effect on his men by saying that the king makes them "passionate" *(erōtikōs ekhein)* to be doing something, while he can say of Socrates that his business is the love trade.[66] And both men enjoy a joke.

Yet Socrates and Cyrus are not exactly the same, either, for Cyrus is certainly not devoted to the life of the mind and Socrates never cares to pursue the life of honor and glory to be found in government. Socrates can always talk with whomever he likes, whenever he likes, and as a thinker he is concerned with the true definitions of things. Cyrus finds to his dismay that the press of government leaves him less time to be with those whose company he desires, his life turns more toward action than toward speculation, and it is inevitably involved in certain processes of deception which cannot be likened to the philosopher's irony.[67]

But Xenophon, both in his Socratic works and in the *Kyroupaideia*, seems intent on underlining the importance of incorporating a particular good within a societal good. Cyrus and Socrates stand not as two opposite poles, public and private, government and philosophy, but as two complements of one reality. Cyrus acts as overt and glorious ruler, Socrates as a ruler of the mind, whose thought ultimately establishes the validity of the *polis* and its proper ordering. Socrates as his particular value gives to the city an intellectual basis which may serve to defend it against its subverters, while Cyrus has as his particular excellence the maintenance of the city against its foes in arms. Socrates masters with words, Cyrus with deeds. Each is crucial to the city; though Xenophon may have considered the life of Socrates "higher" than that of Cyrus because it was its own reward and accordingly less fraught with the temptations of power, nonetheless philosophy's absence in the *Kyroupaideia* does not denigrate the heroic deeds of his Persian monarch. It might even be said that part of the *Kyroupaideia's* charm resides precisely in this fanciful dream of a perfect polity conjured up by a philosopher who knew the peculiar limits of philosophy no less than those of other endeavors.[68]

Indeed it is in the city where both men reveal themselves and manifest their community of interest. If Cyrus as best ruler seeks to inculcate and preserve justice, being himself a seeing law, Socrates dies rather than violate that justice. Similarly both men, as types of an ideal, stand beyond the motley and the mediocrity of the *polis,* and there can be no doubt that in Cyrus' case, as well as in Socrates', Xenophon believed that the nature of the excellent individual had a value the city could fail to appreciate only in its folly. For the city is dependent on its best individuals to provide it with its best direction.[69] Thus both men, not just Socrates, transcend the city, but only the city perverted, the city foolish, the city unjust. In the *Kyroupaideia* it is clear that Xenophon is more interested in a man than an institution; yet he does not mean to invite his readers to a life of solipsism but to the contemplation of how the individual fulfils his excellence in the political, which for one kind of person means attaining the city's rule and working for its just increase.

Cyrus dies, so Xenophon would have it, at home in bed, giving fatherly advice to his sons, quiet and unafraid, endowed with good cheer. But with his death Xenophon's vision ends as well; history returns, even as it had been present at the very beginning. Cyrus' proposal at the end of Book Seven to insure a proper education for the Persians' children is mocked by his own sons' infidelity, as described at the end of Book Eight, to their father's principles. In other words when the great man is gone, the society crumbles; and the chaos depicted at the start of the *Kyroupaideia* returns triumphant at its end.[70] Cyrus believed that by being as upright and just as possible there was little likelihood that his sons would become scoundrels.⁷¹ It was a noble belief, and the only sensible one to act upon. But what the *Kyroupaideia* seems to teach in the end is that noble men remain mortal and their deeds and institutions remain vulnerable to life's randomness. Reality resists perfection. Xenophon could have found little consolation in philosophy, as some would like to say,⁷² because he knew full well what Kambyses taught Cyrus:

> θεοὶ . . ., ὦ παῖ, . . . εἰ δὲ μὴ πᾶσιν ἐθέλουσι συμβουλεύειν, οὐδὲν θαυμαστόν· οὐ γὰρ ἀνάγκη αὐτοῖς ἐστιν ὧν ἂν μὴ θέλωσιν ἐπιμελεῖσθαι.
>
> The gods, . . . my boy, . . . if they do not wish to advise everyone, well, no wonder in that; for there is no necessity upon them to care for those they do not want to.⁷³

Just as the philosopher knew the limited power of words, so Xenophon knows in the *Kyroupaideia* the limited power of deeds. It is not a case of Cyrus' failure to establish an order which will permit his kingdom to continue on after him in prosperity;⁷⁴ it is rather a case of Xenophon's perception that rule such as Cyrus obtained bears within itself a tendency to declination by alluring its wielders with its splendor while destroying in the powerful their sense of responsibility. Cyrus as a young man made the old-fashioned Persian *paideia* into something more dynamic and less concerned with the practice of virtue for its own sake. It is a disturbing possibility that in this very action, which turned Cyrus and his agemates to the winning of honorable renown based upon justice, the *Kyroupaideia* teaches its ultimate lesson.

Gellius preserves a tradition according to which Xenophon wrote the *Kyroupaideia* in reply to the so-called *Republic* of one of his Socratic contemporaries.⁷⁵ It is easy to see the truth behind the legend, if legend it be. For Plato wrote a Socratic dialogue, his king was a philosopher directed towards the realm of forms immutable, eternal, beguiling to contemplate. He could therefore build a polity of optimism. Xenophon, however, did not share such a disdain for the material and this-worldly; his king is not a philosopher, and by the same token his Socrates could admire Themistokles and at least respect Perikles.⁷⁶ Nonetheless perfect polity must have stuck him as a willful delusion; and so in the *Kyroupaideia* he wrote an epic novel whose noble protagonist may—but only may—instruct, though his deeds are as grass. For all its high confidence, for all its mighty exploits, the *Kyroupaideia* retains a poignance Homer would have known, the sad sense that all things pass.

4

TYRANNY

*Toutes les belles paroles sont susceptibles
de plus d'un sens.* — Joubert

Cyrus, after he had conquered Babylon, was quick to realize the problems of governing a captive and hostile population. The first thing he needed was a personal bodyguard because of the enmity between city and master:

> αὕτη δ᾽οὕτως, ἔχοι αὐτῷ ὡς πολεμιωτάτη ἂν γένοιτο ἀνδρὶ πόλις.
>
> it was as hostile to him as the most hostile city could be to a man.[1]

Xenophon stresses their opposition here by juxtaposing the words "man" and "city," but he does not examine it in detail, since Cyrus was not a tyrant. But it is precisely this opposition which Xenophon depicts as the classic feature of tyranny in the *Hiero*, an imaginary conversation between the Sicilian despot Hiero of Syracuse and the poet Simonides. Tyranny was a natural topic for Xenophon to consider, given his interest in the individual, for the tyrant is the perfect example of the man who lives in and of himself without regard for societal *nomoi*.[2] Probably prompted by the rise and fall of Jason in the seventies and the activities of Plato's erstwhile tutee, the Syracusan Dionysios the Younger, in the sixties, the *Hiero* analyzes what happens when one force in the tension between individual and *polis* overextends itself.

The dialogue begins quickly at a moment when the two participants have some leisure time.[3] It should not be surprising that what they say reflects the banter and jest of carefree conversation. Fittingly enough Simonides, who will be proved much the wiser, protests his ignorance of the difference between private and tyrannical life and asks Hiero for enlightenment. When the poet has made some preliminary observations trying to establish that the tyrant is better off than the private man because he has more good things, the tyrant replies:

> Οὐx οὕτως ἔχει, ὦ Σιμωνίδη, ταῦτα, ἀλλ' εὖ ἴσθ' ὅτι μείω πολὺ εὐφραίνονται οἱ τύραννοι τῶν μετρίως διαγόντων ἰδιωτῶν, πολὺ δὲ πλείω καὶ μείζω λυποῦνται.

> Not so, Simonides. Rather, know well that tyrants are much less happy than private citizens who live moderately, and they have many more and many greater troubles.[4]

The rhetoric of this statement should not go unnoticed. The repetition of "much," the emphasis accorded by position in the Greek to an important word like "less," the suspension of "tyrants" to set it off against "private individuals," and the rampant sound echoes, may all be what prompt Simonides to reply that Hiero speaks the unbelievable.[5] No less tell-tale are Hiero's constant use of the first-person pronoun, by which he promotes himself more than the argument,[6] and his fondness for anaphora.[7]

Hiero is quick to point out that the tyrant is worse off than the private man because he can have little confidence that his position, indeed his life will continue. As he insists, what human relationships are pleasant without *pistis* (trust)?[8] Yet the tyrant can be sure of no one, and the whole foundation of a stable system seems undermined. The tyrant is the essentially unfriendly man, he is incapable of what cities prize so highly and what they especially protect in the case of husbands and wives.[9] Far from being a family man, the tyrant, to preserve his position, will stop at killing no one, not brother, not child, not parent.[10]

In fact the tyrant is a kind of warrior, but a warrior who sees as his foes not only foreigners but fellow citizens; and so the war he fights is unending.[11] It is only by continued might that he insures his people's subservience, and it is only by force that he obtains what he needs. But just as there are two sides to every battle, so fear of the tyrant is two-edged; the tyrant himself is victimized by the frightening thought that someone will remove him. Consequently he lives a life of radical isolation, unattended by pleasure, since it is a constant struggle to achieve what is at best only grudging service.[12] Yet Hiero would rather harm himself than be the object of an affection not offered freely.[13] His condition is unnatural. To his sort the gods, with an exquisite sense of justice, give in the afterlife the fate of Tantalos, which was, as that paragon of civic virtue Iskhomakhos reports, the unending fear of dying twice.[14]

The absence of *pistis* in Hiero's regime should induce caution about trusting the sincerity of his remarks. He protests too much. His attempts to persuade Simonides that the life of an *idiōtēs* is preferable to a tyrant's are at times so overwrought that the poet at one point laughs outright.[15] Hiero even attempts to gain his points by flattering the poet's wisdom at the same time as he feigns surprise that a man so wise as he does not see the truth in the tyrant's allegations.[16] When he has disposed of Simonides' various objections, he is eager to continue with his own arguments, as though by an overwhelming accumulation of the horrors of tyranny he will be more convincing about them.[17] His enthusiasm does not, however, trip up his tongue. He puts his dilemma neatly:

> τὸ δὲ φοβεῖσθαι μὲν ὄχλον, φοβεῖσθαι δ' ἐρημίαν, φοβεῖσθαι δὲ ἀφυλαξίαν, φοβεῖσθαι δὲ καὶ αὐτοὺς τοὺς φυλάττοντας, καὶ μήτ' ἀόπλους ἔχειν ἐθέλειν περὶ αὑτὸν μήθ' ὡπλισμένους ἡδέως θεᾶσθαι, πῶς οὐκ ἀργαλέον ἐστι πρᾶγμα;

> Fearing crowds, yet fearing solitude, fearing the absence of guards, yet fearing the very guards, not desiring to have unarmed men about one, yet not viewing armed men with pleasure, how is this not a difficult predicament?[18]

The clever balancing of opposites within each of his phrases, the ever-present anaphora, and the artful variation in the last member of the catalogue belie the very fear which Hiero claims enslaves him. Men afraid do not ask rhetorical questions. Simonides calls Hiero's bluff when he replies to all this how "oh so overly well" the tyrant expresses some things.[19] Hiero's comments are well turned, nice; but his rhetoric fails to convince by its obvious excess. He is mouthing *doxa*, appearances, not realities.

But does the lack of truth reside in Hiero's statements themselves or in his attitude towards them?[20] The conversational setting is, to be sure, a playful debate in which Hiero will uphold his side of the argument no matter what. But it must be realized that the entire discussion is concerned only with a quantitative distinction between the *idiōtēs* and the tyrant, a question of *pleonexia* and *meionexia*, having more and having less.[21] A qualitative difference would seem not to apply; and seen within the context of Xenophon's thought, it becomes clear that the tyrant and the completely private person have in common a lack of political commitment. The discussion is somewhat chimerical insofar as it deliberately avoids the central issue, which is the self-aggrandizing nature of tyranny and not its greater or smaller pleasure quotient vis-a-vis an individual who has remained private rather than public. The features of Hiero's regime are exactly those which Xenophon saw in other tyrannies like the Thirty in Athens:[22] deceit instead of *pistis*, interest in personal, not the common good, with personal self-seeking undone, however, by the very suspicion and confusion it itself engenders. Cyrus, by contrast, never knew these ills; he was a lawful ruler and a father to his subjects. Hiero is Syracuse's master; he cares, not for it, but for himself, as his complaints show. But by his own arguments he makes clear just what Xenophon thought to be the evils of tyranny, especially that the radical assertion of self becomes, paradoxically, a self-contradiction. Hiero, of course, does not truly believe a word he says; the irony is that he is condemned out of his own mouth but does not know it.

Simonides has the one final question, for which Hiero has no clever answer: why is it that nobody ever gives up a tyranny if it is so bad?[23] The tyrant can only reply that he is damned coming and going and that his only advantageous deed is hanging himself.[24] It is Hiero's last attempt to persuade Simonides about the evils of the tyrant's plight. By so doing he has acted the typical tyrant. For he must always do all in his power to dissuade any possible aspirants to tyranny who might become his rivals.

But Simonides does not let Hiero off so easily. He hits at

the heart of the tyrant's elaborate lie—and his political system—when he changes the direction of the conversation. He avers that he can teach Hiero that rule does not preclude endearment and that rule is more advantageous *(pleonektei ge)* than private life.[25] He does not speak so much about tyranny as he does about the more general "rule," and *to arkhein* and *ho arkhōn* occur more frequently in the ensuing remarks than *ho tyrannos*.[26] Simonides introduces that essential distinction between governor and governed which Socrates had made clear to Aristippos,[27] and he argues that only by being at the service of others does the ruler win favor and guard himself against fear and rebellion.[28] Echoing Hesiod, the poet says that the ruler's is an honor from the gods, and therefore citizens are inevitably pleased to be honored in turn by their leaders.[29]

To Hiero's objection that the people's favor will necessarily sour when the police must act, Simonides points out that people are interested in the common good, which protects their private good and which the police defend. Indeed, the citizenry will welcome police presence and even pay for it, since they keep safeguards for less valuable things at their own expense.[30] Simonides' ruler possesses all those qualities the tyrant lacks. He does not compete with private men but with his equals;[31] and in making his city the most prosperous, he is heralded as the victor in the most honorable and outstanding of human contests.[32] Not only does he have friends; his friends are all mankind.[33] As Simonides concludes, in words reminiscent of Cyrus' last advice to his sons, he bids Hiero not to be afraid but to enrich friends and increase the city, since he will thus enrich and increase himself. The poet elaborates this insistence on self-fulfillment through others by asserting finally that Hiero should consider his fatherland as his home, his citizens as his companions, his friends his children, and his children as his very soul.[34]

He invites Hiero, that is to say, to a kind of life he knows Hiero has no intention of following, since it would be impossible for a tyrant to do so and remain a tyrant. It has correctly been stressed that the second part of the *Hiero* is even more rhetorical than the first,[35] for the rule Simonides describes is a fanciful one. It is for this reason that Xenophon casts a poet in the dialogue, being aware that an ideal tyrant is not an ideal but an impossibility, a contradiction in terms. The *Hiero* remains in its second half a *jeu d'esprit*, a whimsical attempt at an improvement whose futility is inescapable. The tyrant is silent at the end of the dialogue which bears his name. Is it because he can make no reply to the vision of Simonides? Or could it be that he has quietly left the scene to return to the rule he enjoys in incorrigible delusion? Be that as it may, his delusion is complemented by Simonides'; for it is Simonides, after all, who first maintains the desirability of tyranny and whose eloquent description makes the institution appear better than it is. Simonides does not express, therefore, the sincere imaginings of Xenophon, nor ought Xenophon to be taken here as conceiving, even in a purely theoretical way, how a government without law could operate successfully. The *Kyroupaideia* presents the ideal of government; the *Hiero* confirms that ideal in a purely negative way, by showing what a good ruler is not. And what he is not is self-aggrandizing.

Xenophon in the *Hiero* presents the tyrant as a warlike figure, suspicious of all and hostile even to those who ought to be most dear. He also examines the warrior spirit in his treatise on the *Constitution of the Lacedaemonians*. The Spartans, of course, were renowned for their military prowess and their devotion to the primary virtues of military life, courage and disciplined obedience. Xenophon in different works actually uses them as examples of that adherence to order which brings victory and leadership over others and for which Sparta merited praise from others of his contemporaries.[36] It is not surprising, therefore, that the *Constitution* has generally been interpreted as a sincere praise of the Spartan way of life by a man who admired both order and bodily rigor, who lived close to the Spartans, and who was the good friend of a Spartan king.

Yet there are anomalies. Various commentators have noted that the praiseworthy life of Iskhomakhos hardly squares with that of the Lacedaemonians; Spartans were not farmers.[37] Moreover Iskhomakhos' concept of justice found its inspiration in the laws of Solon and the royal enactments of Persia, not in the code of the Spartan lawgiver Lykourgos.[38] Furthermore, Xenophon's Socrates, even as he suggests to Perikles *fils* that the Athenians might take a lesson from the Spartans, also remarks that the Athenians would certainly prove superior to them.[39] Finally Cyrus' explicit education against theft, not to mention the *Kyroupaideia*'s presentation of conjugal fidelity and the family, contrasts sharply with prominent features of Spartan life as Xenophon describes them in the *Constitution*.[40] Awareness of these conflicts has elicited the opinion that in the *Constitution* Xenophon was driven to give excessive praise[41] or that the desire to defend "his dear Lacedaemonians" compelled him to employ sophistic reasoning.[42]

The presumption, in other words, that Xenophon was a laconiser has supported an approach to the *Constitution* which turns the simple and restrained Socratic into the opposite of himself, while at the same time, in an abandoning of logic, the treatise is used to confirm Xenophon's philo-Spartan tendencies. It will of course be pointed out that Xenophon's praise is not unadulterated, for in the fourteenth and penultimate chapter of the essay he criticizes the failures of contemporary Sparta and seems to contrast them with the virtues of an earlier time. This chapter has always irked readers, since it spoils the coherence of the rest of the piece, and scholars have employed all the devices of their trade to account for this strange intrusion, from changing the order of the chapters (on no manuscript authority)[43] to impugning the unity of the whole work and positing a different time of composition for the apparently ill-fitting part.[44] But this involved ingenuity cannot satisfy, since if there was anything Xenophon was not, he was not inept at composition.[45] Nor will it be satisfactory to maintain that Xenophon could admire Lykourgos' laws and deplore modern Sparta's departure from them; for Xenophon's was not a mind which contented itself with descriptions of events or statements in an argument without trying to understand their interconnectedness. It is at least more proper to assume as a first hypothesis that Xenophon was as interested in the fundamental cause of this decline as he was in the mere fact of its occurence. Xenophon's criticism in the fourteenth chapter of the *Constitution* will thus be only the most blunt and visible part of an integrated conception of the Spartan system.[46]

To account for the decline, Xenophon's description highlights the Spartans' usurpation of power abroad, their susceptibility to flattery, and their love of lucre. Now it is these things in particular which Lykourgos' laws sought to check. Can their failure to do so on so large a scale be considered as their own indictment? That is to say, the system developed in Sparta may have led almost by definition to the very reality Xenophon, Athens, and the rest of Greece knew and appreciated all too well. Sparta had become an imperialist power under the guise of autonomy for everyone. In the *Hellenika* Xenophon examines, among other things, Sparta's intrinsic inability to play a world role; in the *Constitution* he may have discovered why Sparta naturally turned tyrant in the first place.

Lykourgos' legislation is remarkable for its thorough regulation of all aspects of life in all of life's ages. It attempts to establish rules for everything so that nothing can violate the security of the *polis,* and with Lykourgos' code the connection between individual and city becomes paramount. But in describing the code's chief regulatory purposes, Xenophon strikes a quiet note of doubt concerning the success of such an undertaking. In writing about the approved time for marriage, he remarks that Lykourgos laid down the prime of life as the best period; yet in the next breath he recounts how there were Lykourgan regulations for old men with young wives.[47] Xenophon implies that no matter what the law said was best, complete obedience could not be obtained and that Lykourgos responded to this fact, not by changing the first law, but by creating a new one to cover the deviant situation. The effect of such a proliferation of legislation, however, was ambiguous, for it catered to human will at the same time as it sought to restrain it. Thus when Lykourgos forbade the unlimited intercourse of husband and wife, requiring that they visit each other by stealth, his aim was the procreation of stronger children (the seed would be more robust for not being dissipated),[48] but he was hardly encouraging the mastery of desire as much as he was its potential increase by suppression. In the very opening pages of the *Constitution*, Xenophon, when read attentively, leaves the impression that the Spartan system for all his praise of it was less than perfect; for it abets, even as it seeks to restrain, the unlimited gratification of any passion, so long as detection is avoided. Hence the famous instruction in theft, with stealing punished for being discovered, not for being wrong.[49]

This same perversion of the law of double effect can be seen when Xenophon presents Lykourgos' legislation about money. The great lawgiver attempts to remove the yearning for financial gain and property in a characteristically negative way, by introducing an unwieldy currency of iron bars, which would necessarily hamper, if not hinder, a free commerce and the easy possession of accumulated private wealth.[50] Just previously Xenophon praises the eradication of enslavement to business, yet now he speaks not of its eradication but of its repression. It is also certainly odd that he sees fit to point out that investigators easily discover those who hoard gold and silver.[51] Similarly Spartan fathers are said not to mind their wives bearing sons to other men because difference in paternity will help to eliminate quarrels amongst brothers over the disposition of inheritances.[52] Within the common mess system no one ever goes hungry because many unexpected bounties accrue from hunts and because the wealthy "sometimes" contribute bread.[53] Some Spartans, it seems by Xenophon's own admission, have invested in more than frugality. More than a meal hangs on that "sometimes." Once again Xenophon's simple statement of the facts subtly calls into question his effusive praise. It is not that he disputes the virtue of obedience or civic devotion. Only in the case of Sparta it is becoming more clear that he sees the appearance of virtue and less of its substance.

For virtue, to be real, must be free; ultimately it is a matter of choice, not compulsion. It is therefore necessary to appreciate the rhetoric of Xenophon's explanation for his honoring Lykourgos after he has reported Lykourgos' complaint that the free practice of virtue does not sufficiently aid cities:

> ἐν τῇ Σπάρτῃ ἠνάγκασε δημοσίᾳ πάντας πάσας ἀσκεῖν τὰς ἀρετάς. ὥσπερ οὖν τῶν ἰδιωτῶν διαφέρουσιν ἀρετῇ οἱ ἀσκοῦντες τῶν ἀμελούντων, οὕτω καὶ ἡ Σπάρτη εἰκότως πασῶν τῶν πόλεων ἀρετῇ διαφέρει, μόνη δημοσίᾳ ἐπιτηδεύουσα τὴν καλοκἀγαθίαν. . . . ἐπέθηκε δὲ καὶ τὴν ἀνυπόστατον ἀνάγκην ἀσκεῖν ἅπασαν πολιτικὴν ἀρετήν.

> In Sparta he compelled public practice of every virtue by everyone. Therefore, just as with private citizens those who practice excel in their virtue over those who are negligent, so too Sparta reasonably excels all cities in virtue, being the only one publicly to strive for the noble and the good. . . . Lykourgos also established the compelling compulsion to practice complete political excellence.[54]

The clever juxtaposition of *pantas* and *pasas* (everyone and every), the constant alliteration, the inordinate homoioteleuton, all provoke suspicion that Spartan virtue would not have to be so "advertized," or its alleged simplicity so elaborated, if it were genuine. It must also be noted that even when Xenophon reports Delphi's sanctioning of Lykourgos' code, his praise is uncertain. He says that Lykourgos received an affirmative reply to his query whether it would be better or not for the Spartans to obey his laws,[55] but Xenophon is silent about whether Lykourgos ever asked the Oracle if his laws were good in themselves. Lykourgos called his laws *pythokhrēstois* (delivered by the Oracle), but Xenophon calls the whole undertaking a *mekhanēma*. Was it merely a "plan," or was it a "scheme"? Was Lykourgos devoted to piety or to the skillful use of piety, knowing the political value of fear of the divine?[56]

This blend of compulsion divine and human underpins the structure of Spartan *paideia* and its emphasis on punishment. Xenophon portrays the drill master only as a severe corrector and says that in this man's absence someone else is always on hand "to punish if they [the youths] should make a mistake."[57] There is a prefect system amongst the boys, so that they will never want for a commander,[58] while the older men, by being compelled to hunt and practice soldiering, are even in their maturity not to be *autonomous*, independent.⁵⁹

Yet it is precisely as the defenders of autonomy that the Spartans present themselves, and it is this same autonomy which Xenophon criticizes them for violating in the *Constitution's* fourteenth chapter. Now either Xenophon did not notice the striking contradiction between his praise for Spartan submission to command and his own stated historical awareness that they proved anything but submissive, or he must be seen as questioning the ultimate value of Spartan customs, even as he seemingly honors them. How can freedom be protected by a people who equate freedom with license? This is the crucial point. The system of Lykourgos certainly succeeds admirably in checking the ambitions of Spartans, but it may be wondered whether it removed them. Lykourgos holds back from wrong the citizens for whom he legislates; he does not positively direct them to do right. Xenophon saw that the Spartans' addiction to flattery abroad ought not to surprise. It is not that they hear only criticism at home and revel in delicious independence when away; rather it is the flowering of a desire for flattery which has always been present, seeking its chance for gratification, just as the Spartan youth seeks for the right moment to commit a theft.

The Lykourgan code catches itself in a dilemma. It inculcates strict obedience to the dictates of the polis and unquestioning observance of commands, but at the same time it recognizes that good soldiering requires initiative and a developed ability to deceive. Xenophon goes on at length about the military rigor of Sparta and even apologizes for his loquacity by stressing that the Spartans leave nothing military unattended.⁶⁰ Yet the care for war has unfortunate consequences. Development of ingenuity and cunning is one thing, but how channel such talents in a state where justice is not taught?⁶¹ Again a conflict arises, from Xenophon's own statements, between his praise and his clear condemnation. For all of Sparta's emphasis on law, it does not teach its children the value of law but only the fear of it. The most cunning and militarily useful Spartan, in fact, can conceivably be the most unjust man in the city, provided his clever violation of laws remains undetected. In achieving military preparedness, Lykourgos fails to distinguish the nature of war and the enemy from the nature of friends and the city. Spartans, as Xenophon is not loathe to report, fight with one another as if they were foes rather than fellow citizens, living at odds with one another and perpetrating thefts on one another.[62]

It is also of a piece with this warrior spirit that family life is practically nonexistent. It must have been no easy feat for a Spartan father to know which children were his own, since promiscuity was rampant and adultery no crime.[63] Eugenics was all that officially mattered. By directing all attention away from private interest, Lykourgos removed what Xenophon, as his other works attest, knew to be an important civic institution because it could engender in the young a sense of obligation and indebtedness to others which he felt essential to a proper civic life. The Spartan citizen is brought up devoid of such indebtedness; he even learns to fight by treating his comrades as his (albeit temporary) foes. He is taught obedience while encouraged to disobey the law; he is taught submission and aggression all at once.

It thus becomes clear how Sparta can be at one and the same time a government founded on the restraint of individual freedom and a power which by self-aggrandizement violated other cities' autonomy. For what was to keep Sparta and the Spartans from self-aggrandizement when removed from the checks at home or when the warrior city and its citizens suddenly found themselves without equally powerful enemies to fear outside? The history of Sparta as Xenophon describes it in the critical chapter of the *Constitution* was not the result of power corrupting but the inevitable upshot of Lykourgos' system from the start. Inured to obedience, the Spartans floundered in authority; taught that property was everybody's possession, that theft was acceptable if undetected, they quite naturally did not hesitate to enjoy openly what at home was done in secret. Sparta, the warrior *polis*, knew nothing of that friendly and peaceful spirit found in other cities. Its citizens punished one another, fought with one another, stole from one another; nowhere does Xenophon say they were friends to one another. No wonder peace turned to dust under the influence of these men and liberty to tyranny. The world became the theatre for their exercises, the stage on which they revealed how rigor and obedience without justice lead to self-aggrandizement, how internal repression is transmuted into foreign aggression.

Xenophon begins the *Constitution* with the statement that he wonders how it was possible for as thinly populated a state as Sparta to achieve so much power, but then he quickly says he no longer wonders after he appreciated the city's Lykourgan institutions. His lack of wonder suits a city where the wonder of philosophy is absent and emphasis is laid on the development of the *sōma*, not the *psychē*. His description of the supposedly ideal conduct of Spartan youths as they walk, their silence the silence of stone statues and their gaze riveted straight as a bronze's,[64] suggests they are automatons, the image of men, not the reality. They know how to act in only one way, and free innovation, even in battle affairs, is as foreign to them as the world outside their city. Xenophon says they look at their feet.[65] How different was the flexibility of Xenophon, who helped get ten thousand Greeks safely out of Persia, how far removed from the sobriety of Sparta was his own gentle charm.

Now there is one sort of gentility which manages with elegant charm never to offend. It is akin to the rhetorical style which manages to say one thing and mean another. Irony, as an ancient oratorical treatise points out, does not have to proceed by sarcasm and mockery; it can also use urbanity *(asteismos)* to effect in laughing at the pomposity of another.[66] Thus it demonstrates to the self-important how they should act, at the same time that it economically criticizes their conduct. Isokrates in his *Panathenaikos* provides an example of such skill when he describes how a former student discovered that the object of his oration was not its apparent praise of Athens, but something more hidden, clear save the ephors.⁷⁵ Here is the rub. Sparta can not afford a strong and independent king because such a monarch would be too much an individual. Consequently, it compels its kings to swear an oath that they will observe the laws:

> for no tyrannical ideas were desired in the kings nor any power-envy in the citizens.⁷⁶

But Sparta is caught in its own trap. Those who oversee the laws and to whom the kings make their oath are, in fact, the masters. Xenophon thus calls the ephors tyrants;⁷⁷ for the *Constitution* too, like the *Hiero*, is an essay against tyranny, perhaps a reply to a work of the same name written by a man for whom Xenophon had little use, Kritias, one of the Thirty.⁷⁸

So Sparta honored its kings as heroes, but, appropriately, only when they died.⁷⁹ The hexameter with which the treatise concludes has always attracted attention. Its epic and spondaic quality evokes a heroism which never was because it never could have been:

> ἀλλ' ὡς ἥρωας
> τοὺς Λακεδαιμονίων βασιλεῖς προτετιμήκασι.
>
> but like heroes
> they hold in honor the kings of the Lacedaemonians.

But something is wrong with the verse. Either Xenophon could not write a better hexameter than a mediocre student of verse composition or the beat in the last two and a half feet is deliberately clumsy, as clumsy as this work's whole laudation. It limps.

5
THE ACTIVE LIFE

La gloire est compatible avec le vice. . . . J'avoue . . . que ce vif aiguillon fait entreprendre de grandes choses, mais il ne s'ensuit pas que ces grandes choses soient bonnes.
—Chapelain

The Spartan king Agesilaos was lame in one leg and walked with a limp. Xenophon's encomium in his honor, however, never mentions this, just as it passes over in silence the oracle against a limping monarchy current at his accession.[1] Such reticence, which extends to the king's mental imperfections as well, suits the *Agesilaos'* thoroughly delicate nature. Here, by contrast with the more forthright *Hellenika*, physical flaws and flaws of character and policy are forgotten, criticism is eschewed, and every rhetorical device is fully employed to make deeds more illustrious which, if viewed impartially, might seem less worthy of praise.[2] Xenophon in thus consciously improving his own historical record cannot be imagined to have expressed most completely in the encomium his own thoughts either about Agesilaos himself or about the kind of life Agesilaos pursued so energetically.

The *Agesilaos* is, moreover, the work of a friend acknowledging the very friendliness which so often animated the Spartan king. It was to Agesilaos that Xenophon owed his estate in Skillous, where he lived out so much of his exile from Athens; and it was with Agesilaos that a chance acquaintance, formed in Asia Minor, strengthened to an abiding bond which Xenophon must have appreciated all the more if, as is probable, his own city had already officially banished him. Xenophon's sense of gratitude was great; but it was a debt owed to his friend, not to his friend's city. As

Agesilaos once told the Persian satrap Pharnabazos, friends from different cities will fight for their fatherlands against one another and even kill one another, if that is needed.[3] So Xenophon admired Agesilaos the individual who was a Spartan, not Agesilaos *the* Spartan individual; and so in his old age, restored to his native home he came to write,[4] upon the death of the king, words of praise which also illuminate those qualities of royal character on which he so often meditated.

It is Agesilaos' noble blood, fittingly enough, which Xenophon emphasizes first. He is, of course, following the standard procedure of an encomium when he begins with the Spartan king's lineage,[5] but his treatment is more than perfunctory. For Xenophon wishes to make clear that his friend was not a man out of nowhere but that he was an individual who was part of a past and a past whose special lustre, though deserving of praise, was not an excuse for complacence but a model for action. Sparta's kings had always acted in the interests not of themselves but of their city, and never did they attempt to obtain greater powers *(meizonōn ōrhekhthēsan)*[6] than they had received originally. The individual king, his family, and his *polis* form, in other words, a unit in which every member reinforces the other to the advantage of each and the detriment of none. In this way the city and the monarchy endured as the most stable polity in Greece, for stability was possible only through the absence of self-seeking ambition and the lust for more.[7] Xenophon thus sees in Agesilaos a man defined by city and family, who is inevitably imbued with a sense of limit, the sense that his actions are directed by other than his own desires and aimed at something besides his own satisfaction. As Xenophon remarks later, nothing Agesilaos did failed to reveal that he was a lover of his city.[8]

This sense of limit underlies all that Xenophon sees in his friend and unifies all the diversity of the king's deeds and virtues. Agesilaos never engages in wars of imperialist aggression. His campaigns in Asia Minor are undertaken to free the Greeks from the Persians; and his return home, highlighted by the battle of Koroneia, is seen as a loyal response to the orders of the Spartan government.⁹ In financial dealings he has a reputation for being not only fair but also absolutely uninterested in venal gain, for he prefers nobly to have less *(meionektein)* than unjustly to have more *(pleon ekhein)*.¹⁰ The only thing he is content to have more of *(pleonektōn)*¹¹ is not wealth or power, but hard work, while the charm which pervades his entire character is the manifestation of a contentment with the simple and an aversion from the excessive and extravagant.¹² Agesilaos is a man who is constantly concerned to do exactly what is required of him, either as general, king, or servant of the gods. His trustworthiness and fidelity to compacts further illustrate, therefore, his passion for the proper and particular. He does not mean as king "to monarchize, be feared, and kill with looks":

> for though honor and power were his, and sovereignty in addition to these, . . . one did not see in him boastfulness but could have recognized, without seeking, a familial affection *(to philostorgon)* and desire to help friends.¹³

This comparison of Agesilaos' rule to a family relationship is not an idle piece of warm praise. It reaffirms Xenophon's fundamental insight into Agesilaos' character, where the claims of family and city regulate individual desire. Agesilaos, in Xenophon's eyes, does not guide his actions according to a principle of self-aggrandizement but in the spirit of openness, trust, and mutual aid and protection which can prevail in the relationship of parent and child. The analogy is important, finally, because it makes clear just that insistence on simplicity, the avoidance of the grandly majestic, which paradoxically rendered the Spartan king's success so impressive. Because Agesilaos did not hold himself aloof, he was, as Xenophon remarks, longed after when he left Asia Minor not only as a good leader but also as a friend and father.¹⁴

The sense of limit underlying Agesilaos' rule, its close and, as it were, familial rather than distant quality, also characterizes Agesilaos' justice. Always faithful to oaths sworn by the gods, he does not permit his victorious army to work injustice by violating his defeated foes' rights of sanctuary.¹⁵ By the same token, he does not allow captured enemies to be treated as men who are unjust but as men who are human beings.[16] He is always glad when the just are rewarded more than the unjust, a thought befitting not only a moral man but also one who considers every action in terms of what it requires and not with a view to the gain it may bring at the expense of others.[17] Indeed he regulates his life so carefully even in financial matters that "he was never compelled for money's sake to do anything unjust."[18] But most important of all, and what Xenophon finds most praiseworthy about him, is his constancy of character when confronted with enormous wealth and power. Agesilaos does not embark on a personal quest for glory but continues to adhere to the commands of his city. His kingship is as great as it is because he is still king of himself. He returns to Greece showing clearly:

> how he would not take the whole world in place of his fatherland, nor new friends in place of old, nor shameful and easy gains instead of noble and just ones, even if they involved dangers.[19]

After the battle at Koroneia, Agesilaos reveals how he has chosen

> instead of being the greatest man in Asia, at home to have the customary ways rule and to have them rule him.[20]

Once again, therefore, the city, this time by its laws and decrees, even as it puts a check on the king's actions, enables him to realize all the more the true nature of his royalty.

It is this kind of royalty in limits which men might tend to dismiss as being unremunerative in power or wealth or as being downright shabby. Xenophon therefore consciously opposes to the frugal excellence of Agesilaos the sumptuous splendor of the Persian king in order to show up the latter as a sham and a mockery, as the mere appearance of monarchy and not its substance. Unlike Agesilaos, the Great King flees the cold and the hot, "through weakness of soul imitating the life not of good men but of the weakest animals."[21] He hides himself from others and is difficult of access, as if to strengthen his claims to power;[22] and although the Persian is always seen in the *Agesilaos* as an enslaver, there is a clear suggestion that the weak and effeminate eastern ruler is no less a slave than his own subjects, because he himself is in thrall to pleasure and to a bogus sense of his own might. The Spartan king, on the other hand, can endure all toils and is subject to no vainglory. He is a free man, whose characteristic deed in the encomium is to defeat the Persians and to bring freedom to the Greeks they sought to master. Ever the Socratic, Xenophon seeks in the *Agesilaos* to define "what is a king" and to suggest that royalty, if genuine, is not founded upon license but limit. The Persian, for all his appearance of power, is an *alazōn*, which is to say, an imposter who claims to be greater than he really is.[23]

It thus gradually becomes clear that the *Agesilaos* is not concerned merely to preserve the memory of one man's deeds and virtues. While it is, of course, true that the events of Agesilaos' life explain in one way Xenophon's inclusion of his encounters with the Persians, it would nevertheless be an incomplete vision of the work which failed to see how it operates simultaneously on a level which transcends the simply chronological. Xenophon seems intent on trying to understand what lies behind an action when he remarks that Agesilaos' character will best become clear from his deeds, while his virtues, when examined, will reveal what inspired all that he did.[24] Neither inner nor outer reality are by themselves sufficient for an understanding of the Spartan king; the two facets must be appreciated together. Xenophon is paying more than a personal debt or private homage in writing his encomium; for not only does he see in Agesilaos an individual embodiment of various abstractions like justice, piety, wisdom, and patriotism, but also an exemplar, a kind of standard according to which other men may direct their action no less than they do according to the demands of justice and fidelity:

> The excellence of Agesilaos would seem to me to be a noble model *(kalon . . . paradeigma)* for those wishing to practice nobility.[25]

The *Agesilaos* thus constantly operates on two levels, the chronological and the timeless, the literal and the emblematic.

In seeking to praise his friend, therefore, Xenophon has also managed to find what is praiseworthy in a life devoted to *aretē* and *doxa*, exploits of excellence and fame,[26] and to find an inherent antagonism between this kind of heroism and the claims of the self, between true heroism and the heady trappings of power. In genuine nobility, as he sees it, there is something essentially Greek which the Persian can only ape but never achieve, if only because the Greek is free. Excellence to be real must be willed; and it is fitting that in Agesilaos' life Xenophon sees little that results from the domination of passion or chance. Luck does not make a man essentially better as a general or an economist even if it may win him an occasional fight or find him an occasional treasure.[27] So too before describing Koroneia, Xenophon explicitly says he does not praise Agesilaos for being a man who engaged in a glorious but otherwise senseless battle against vastly superior numbers. The forces were, on the contrary, evenly matched; it was Agesilaos' planning and ability to command that merit honor, and anything else is foolishness.[28]

It is also shortly after Koroneia, at Corinth, that Agesilaos expresses his sorrow over the fratricidal warfare of the Greeks, how the numbers of fallen could better have fought against the Persians.[29] Though this remark and Xenophon's juxtaposing elsewhere the Greek and Persian monarchy might suggest a political slant, propaganda is not Xenophon's aim. He has in mind something larger and more noble. Xenophon the encomiast is interested in something more abiding than time's encomium; like a Socratic he praises what is eternally memorable, what will live forever.[30] The *Agesilaos* does not urge men to an assault on Persia so much as it urges them, if bent on renown, to consider the self-mastery of the Spartan king. This alone can bring that lasting personal glory some might have thought possible only apart from the city, perhaps even outside Greece in Persia itself.

It may well be wondered what Agesilaos would have thought of his friend's tribute; he might barely have recognized himself. He was a man of deeds, not thoughts, and it is precisely in a "thoughtful" way that Xenophon chooses to assess him. It may be, after all, that the deception of an encomium, as apparent and expected as it is, can not fully conceal the difference between friend and friend, between one kind of aretē and another. Agesilaos idealized is the perfect man of affairs, but he is not necessarily the best man. For Xenophon does not suggest that his actions flow from first principles rigorously examined, nor does he ever allow to intrude the problem posed by obedience to the demands of a *polis* when those demands are unjust. He does not mean to denigrate Agesilaos' glory; indeed it is thanks to Xenophon that Agesilaos will always outshine the Persian. Yet Xenophon finds fidelity to the city and benefaction to others most fully realized not in a king of royal birth but in a man of lesser station, whose only exploit is to bear witness to the ancient laws of Athens and to reveal their subversion by others through his constant inquiries into the truth. Though sharing much in common with Agesilaos in Xenophon's mind, Socrates nevertheless stands apart from him because he is endowed with an understanding of heroic renown and patriotism which goes beyond the deceits of an encomium, however mild.

* * *

Like Agesilaos, Xenophon had personal knowledge of the Persians; but unlike the king, his encounter with them did not reveal his perfect citizenship or even necessarily his good sense. He reports in the *Anabasis* that he makes up his mind to serve with the younger Cyrus after a friend, Proxenos, has enticed him to join by promising that he can make Cyrus Xenophon's friend, the Cyrus whom Proxenos thinks "more important for himself than his fatherland."[31] When Xenophon seeks Socrates' advice, his teacher cautions him about the dangers of offending his fellow Athenians, whom Cyrus has helped to defeat in the Peloponnesian War. Yet when Xenophon inquires of the Oracle, the question he puts—how will things turn out best on the journey—shows that he is determined to go. He has little hesitation, and even Socrates can not break his resolve.[32] Xenophon's account of the results of the decision, the *Anabasis*, may thus be taken as the most important of his non-Socratic works, since it shows the consequences of an imprudent personal rejection of Socrates and of the city which nurtured them both. As a resolute, vigorous, and headstrong young man he seeks out a life of adventure, away from the city, in the company of another friend, who is, as Xenophon makes clear, a student of the sophist Gorgias of Leontinoi, and eager "to do great things."[33]

Cyrus is just the sort to appeal to such men. As his obituary reveals, he was an extravagant and dashing man who searched for the dangerous and grappled with it hand-to-hand.[34] It is said to his credit that he was lavish with his wealth, sharing it liberally amongst others, who became his fast friends and who were encouraged to make more money on their own. Nor was he an unjust man, since he always rewarded those who did right and so further insured men's observance of what was proper.[35] It is not surprising, therefore, that everyone who knew him considered him, of all the Persians after his great namesake, the most royal and most deserving of empire.[36]

Yet his regal nature has a more chilling side. Those not won over to his justice and authority are punished with an extravagant severity which must have repelled as well as warned his Hellenic comrades as they saw people along the highways blind or lacking hands or feet.[37] Open and friendly as Cyrus may be, his largesse never seems to rise above the aims of simple self-advancement. He is the center and the circumference, who is all and contains all but who never seems to win to himself men who think of more than money. Cyrus is the ultimate mercenary, and it is mercenaries he attracts to his service. Though most royal of Persians, he is not inevitably most royal of men. So enamoured of the material and its uses as he is, it is not surprising that he should yearn for the throne of another, that this prince, for all his apparent justice, can yet become a rebel and seek to take his own brother's life.[38]

There is, then, in Cyrus a certain deceptiveness, beneath the swashbuckling bravery a designing aloofness. Not for nothing does he keep his truest thoughts to himself and effect a masterpiece of deceit by enlisting his army of Greeks and gaining men like Proxenos and the young Xenophon. They do not know where they are really going until they have gone too many stathmoi and parasangs to turn back. Geography has mastered them; demands for more money help ease their entrapment.[39] Most of them, Xenophon says, did not join Cyrus out of poverty but because they were attracted by reports of Cyrus' excellence; they hoped to profit by his generosity and return home with riches, "hearing that the others with Cyrus were doing quite well for themselves."[40] They saw the allure of *aretē* and did not think twice before succumbing to it.[41] But allure was all it was, and for many it was fatal.

It is remarkable how much guile and how much deceitful speech occur in the narrative of the march to Kounaxa. Klearkhos, Cyrus' confidant, resorts to tears and protestations of devotion for his men in an effort to win their favor and to keep them on the campaign against Artaxerxes, although they should know him to be a rough and war-loving man who strikes his men unreasonably.[42] Cyrus himself is an expert at cozening, of course. When two Greeks actually desert him, causing some of their forsaken comrades to wish them captured as cowards and some to pity them if apprehended, Cyrus proclaims his goodwill toward those who left, thereby increasing for himself the goodwill of those who remained.[43] Yet earlier a Greek has realized that to leave Cyrus, even with his prior consent, is a risky business; for he can sink their transports with his triremes, and any guide he provides for a land march can well lead them to where there is no return.[44]

A small incident in Babylonia, where Xenophon sees fit to recall an example of Persian discipline, should also have prompted doubts in more minds than it did about Cyrus as a commander, once all knew his purpose. One day some wagons become stuck in mud, halting the forward march, which has to proceed swiftly if Artaxerxes is to be taken by surprise and his defeat rendered easy. Cyrus and his best and wealthiest men investigate the situation, then Cyrus despatches some soldiers to remedy the problem. But Cyrus thinks they are working too slowly and "as in anger" *(hōsper orgēi)* he orders his companions, finery and all, to jump in the mud and help get the wagons out.[45] There may be more than a little humor in the scene of these begrimed dandies sloshing in the mud, while Cyrus remains apart, ever the Persian prince. How different the action of Klearkhos the Greek general, who thinks nothing of getting down into the dirt with the men subordinate to him, or, later, of Xenophon who dismounts from his horse to walk like an infantryman or is seen by his men half-naked in the cold, chopping wood.[46] Cyrus at no time seems to mix with his men, to be available to them; never is he called, like the ideal commander of the *Agesilaos*, a father to them. He was not that kind of man; he did not fraternize, as Artaxerxes could affirm.

But the scene suggests more. When the Persian nobles rush off headlong to obey their leader, running as if they were in a race, Xenophon calls it an example of *eutaxia*.[47] Does he mean that he admires their immediate response to the order, or is he perhaps being slightly sarcastic in calling their racing from all sides "good formation"? For it is precisely good formation that Cyrus' Persian troops lack at the crucial battle, Kounaxa, and the same impatience which causes Cyrus' angry command about the stuck wagons finally causes his undoing. When Artaxerxes does not appear to fight at the time Cyrus thinks he will, Cyrus becomes careless and marches with his defenses down and his troops in disarray *(anatetaragmenon)*.[48] When battle is finally joined, the scene in his army is one of utter confusion:

> Then indeed there was much confusion; for the Greeks and everyone were thinking that the King would fall upon them straightway, when they were out of order.[49]

Cyrus himself, as soon as he sees close up his long-awaited brother, cannot control himself, shouting out excitedly, "I see the man," and protected by only a few, he charges off against him. And there Cyrus and his retinue perish.[50]

It is curious that in relating Cyrus' death Xenophon should pause to describe, in a narrative otherwise remarkably swift, the scimitar and other finery belonging to a loyal servant of the prince, who died with him.[51] Xenophon leaves one final and lasting image of the wealth of the dashing and seemingly heroic Persian rebel and of the way he could use it to reward even a faithful attendant, let alone a noble. But at the same time Cyrus and his Persians have lost, their fine garb and gorgeous weaponry count for nothing. At Kounaxa a truth finally emerges from the preceding deceit; only the Greek mercenaries, unpaid but disciplined, achieve victory. Cyrus earlier admires them for their freedom and sees that it has nothing to do with money:

> Be therefore men worthy of the freedom you possess and for which I count you fortunate. For know well that I would prefer freedom to all the things I own, many times over.[52]

It is fitting, too, that Xenophon should close his obituary of Cyrus with the notice that Ariaios, a companion of Cyrus, flees the battle as soon as he sees the prince is dead. He and his force become thereafter minions of Artaxerxes, when before they had been "most loyal to Cyrus."[53] Doubtless they reckon it is time to look for a new donor of gifts. Their action reveals that profound slavery to things from which not even the most royal Persian is free.

Kounaxa makes clear to the Greeks the value of their discipline and freedom, but they do not yet correctly apprehend the true nature of their situation. Appeals to them from Artaxerxes to surrender their arms only elicit in response gnomic truths such as "rule is the prerogative of those who conquer in battle" or "conquerors do not surrender."[54] The deceit of earlier days has taken on a new character, as the Greeks now attempt to fool themselves, confident in their own excellence. When a Greek in Artaxerxes' employ, Phalinos, informs them of their real predicament, deep as they are in Persian territory, lost, without supplies, greatly outnumbered, he factually rebuts the mildly intellectual but totally pointless queries of Gorgias' student Proxenos about the workings of the King's mind.[55] He also disappoints Klearkhos' hope that he, a Greek who knows the King, will advise the Greeks to disregard Artaxeres.[56] One other interlocutor, an Athenian named Theopompos, perhaps voices best the heady heroism of the army, for which the emissary has only scorn. On arms and aretē alone did the Greeks rely, and with them, Theopompos proclaims, they can fight for the possessions of the Persians. Phalinos laughs:

> You seem like a philosopher, young man, and you speak not without charm. Yet know that you are a fool if you can imagine that your excellence could ever vanquish the might of the King.[57]

Only gradually do the Greeks come to appreciate their situation and the need for sensible action. But even so, they express their understanding with a swagger; the King must be attacked, they insist to Klearkhos:

> for he will not willingly desire us, having got back to Greece, to announce how we, the number that we are, conquered the King at his very doors and got away having made him a laughingstock.[58]

Klearkhos knows the more sober realities yet seems incapable of developing a successful plan of withdrawal. In fact his position as commander is something he obtained only because no one else had any experience. As Xenophon shows in his character sketches, the Greek generals lack some essential qualities of leadership; and the misfortunes and uncertainty of the Greeks after Kounaxa are the result not only of their own bravado but also of the poor direction they received. None of the commanders can accurately assess the situation and get the force out, neither the naive Proxenos nor the unsubtle Klearkhos. The latter turns to the gods, hoping for answers better sought in deliberation. When a stranger, who turns out subsequently to have been suborned by the enemy, reveals some seemingly disastrous news, the Spartan is "thrown into terrible confusion" *(etarakhthē sphodra)*[59] and becomes afraid. His last address to Tissaphernes is a masterpiece of quandary and pious doubletalk; at his poor wit's end he seeks support in bogus faith.[60] In accepting the satrap's ominous invitation to a parley, he merely acquiesces to a greater master in deceit. For Tissaphernes' final speech to Klearkhos and the Greeks before the slaughter of the captains and arrest of the generals is irony perfected to vengeance; his passion to be trusted by them, he assures the Greeks, is what has kept him from destroying them.[61]

Tissaphernes' assault upon the Greek commanders is considered and astute. It is only when deprived of so many leaders that the Greeks finally understand fully their predicament, going over in their minds the very things Phalinos and Klearkhos have told them before.[62] But what impresses them most in their despair is the thought that they will never again look upon their fatherlands, parents, wives, and children.[63] The very things they have so blithely left behind in the pursuit of adventure and fortune are now the very ones that will inspire them to acts of heroism which monetary reward could not induce. Now they begin to realize their nature as Greeks, and they expel from their midst anyone who dishonors his fatherland with counsels of submission.[64] New leaders take over, Xenophon among them, elected, not appointed by fiat; and plans are discussed in assembly, not kept secret or delivered by generals from on high.

The army, in other words, discovers its hope in its freedom and begins to act in accord with it. At this time, too, deception begins to vanish; the inspiring speeches of Xenophon, designed to lift flagging spirits, are the first in the *Anabasis*, for all their rhetoric, to be free of mendacity or uncertainty. Though he may minimize the dangers confronting him and his fellows, he never lies; and once he has succeeded in giving them a sense of direction, persuasive harangues become less frequent and less long. Speech, once the vehicle of deceit, gives way to action, the quest for glory to the quest for the simple goal of home and homeland. A sense of direction has been achieved.

Xenophon considers the essential requirement of the retreat to be good leadership, and from the beginning he displays a concern that competent commanders be put in charge. His first act, even before addressing the despairing troops, is to rouse the surviving officers and to arrange for the replacement of those arrested or dead. As he tells them, nothing honorable or good can ever happen without a commander, especially in war. In good order *(eutaxia)* is salvation; lack of discipline has already destroyed many.[65] When addressing the rank and file he urges them to be more orderly and obedient to their officers than they have been before.⁶⁶ He shows himself from the first as a man confident in the success which structure and organization bring and consequently as a man devoted to preserving this ordered system.

Many have observed how the retreating army resembles a *polis*, and its operation lends itself to valuable sociological study.⁶⁷ Nor can there be any doubt that its cohesiveness as a group aided it in its successful march to the sea. It is fascinating also to observe how different abilities are used: Cretans make good archers, and Rhodians good slingers.⁶⁸ All work together for the common good under the guidance of commanders who can push forward no matter what, like the Spartan Kheirisophos, or who can quickly contrive stratagems to surmount special hindrances, like the Athenian Xenophon.⁶⁹ It is, in fact, remarkable that Xenophon reports only one real falling out between him and the chief commander, for they were very dissimilar men.

But it is Xenophon himself who, more than any other, seems to embody the highest purpose of the force. Though only a rearguard officer, he gives the impression that he was everywhere. He is the man who keeps the army together in the snows of Armenia, who is always available to them for conversation day or night, who is called "father" and "benefactor."⁷⁰ Above all he is the man who will not let them forget their goal like the men of Odysseus who ate the lotus.⁷¹

But if Xenophon saves them from the Persians and the elements, he can not save them from themselves. Their joy at reaching the sea makes them forget that the sea was not their true goal. Thinking all their troubles are over, they celebrate games as though they have made a conquest.⁷² Kheirisophos is greeted joyously when he proposes to go to his friend, the Spartan admiral Anaxibios, for ships to carry the army back to their fatherland.⁷³ One man from the rank and file, tired of walking and carrying, expresses the happy thoughts of all:

> I yearn, now that I have finished with those toils, since we have reached the sea, to sail the rest of the way and stretched out like Odysseus to arrive in Greece.⁷⁴

Xenophon now confronts a folly *(aphrosunē)*⁷⁵ which becomes more and more destructive to that very structure he has worked so hard to preserve. His first proposals about taking necessary precautions while they wait for Kheirisophos' return the men greet with a bored response that Xenophon captures in the dully repeated phrase *edoxe kai tauta* (motion passed), a sharp contrast to their joyous and enthusiastic reception of Kheirisophos shortly before.[76] More and more the men look to their own private interests, and the army's discipline falls apart. On one occasion they are even surprised by an enemy and routed into a disorderly retreat, which only gives the foe added encouragement. This, as Xenophon quietly observes, had never happened before.[77] Envoys and messengers are no longer immune from the physical assaults of disgruntled individuals who act only on their own authority.[78] The men have become like rabid dogs,[79] and Xenophon's insistence on reason only makes him the object of their attacks. His fellow officers turn on him as well, as each vies with the other for supreme command. In search of popular favor, one of them tries to please his men by irresponsibly giving them everything they want.[80]

The structure thus crumbles both at the top and the bottom; and the army antagonizes the local population, even attempting to take Greek cities by storm. Such brigandage costs them almost three thousand lives in the end.[81] What is the cause? The divided army's reunion after Xenophon's group has helped another unit out of difficulty is suggestive. Then the men "were glad to see each other and welcomed each other like brothers."[82] The *Anabasis* implies that only adversity is enough to keep these men together; without danger they go their own way. In fact even on the march to the sea some men were out to get an advantage over their comrades, as Xenophon reveals when justifying some disciplinary actions he took.[83] The breakdown of the army is only the natural outcome of its own nature. It begins as a chance assemblage of men, with no strong ties of city or family among them. They are all out for profit, and this is apparent as soon as the men feel safe from mortal danger. It is a fitting conclusion that, far from returning home to Greece, these mercenaries once again march up-country against their old foe Tissaphernes. To have imagined they were a *polis* in any real sense was a delusion, and therefore the *Anabasis* does not so much present a record of the mutability of things as it does the tendency of all things to manifest finally their genuine selves.

What is truly remarkable, however, is Xenophon's reaction. Constantly trying to work against the disruption of the force, he is ever more on the defensive before it. He gets next to nothing as reward for his labors and yet seems convinced that he can make an enduring polity out of this clearly temporary grouping of men. He can even conceive, almost pathetically, of establishing a colony on a particularly favorable site, only to be jeered at by an army still insisting it wants to get to Greece. What he thinks is revealing:

> he thought it would be a glorious thing to increase the territory and power of Greece if the men established a city. And it seemed to him it would be a great city as he thought over the number of the men and the people living in the Pontic area.[84]

Xenophon still has a mind set on glorious exploit. Like the men's, his nature has not changed from the time he first joined Cyrus' expedition. Later on he can comment on how hard it will be when the actions of some deprive all of the praise and honor *(epainou kai timēs)* they thought to get in Greece and cause them to be considered the inferior of their countrymen.[85] Not surprisingly when he is offered the post of supreme commander, he desires to accept, for he thinks of the greater honor he will have before his friends and the greater name he will have before the city; last of all he thinks he may be capable of doing some good for the army.[86]

Xenophon is the victim of his own delusion. The army he helped form into a successfully functioning unit he misconstrues as something lasting that can bring him renown. In trying to keep it together he is attempting the impossible. It is even doubtful if he fully appreciates what a city is. In his calculations for his colony he only adds up the numbers who will inhabit it, all soldiers, while his eagerness to march with Cyrus in the first place seems to suggest that he considers his native city both as a place he can lightly leave and the place where his own glory may shine. There is no notion of the intricacies of civic justice and civic life. It all seems so easy. He has not yet learned to understand the lesson of Socrates, who stays in the city through radical democracy and radical oligarchy, trying always to be true to its ancient laws and seeking to discover and elucidate through conversation and reason what are the basic principles which give the *polis* life.

This is not to say, however, that Xenophon is no better than the men around him, that he is just some sort of glorified mercenary. His poverty proves that money did not ultimately matter; and, as he tells Seuthes, he considers no possession more honorable for a man, especially a leader, than excellence, justice, and nobility.[87] The difficulty lies in his slowness to learn that the way in which he pursues these virtues is one of toil fraught with reversals. Although his defense of his actions before Seuthes and the army rings true, it reveals his failure to comprehend how the men could turn on him or Seuthes betray him. He sarcastically calls his fellow Greeks "most gifted with memory of everything" when he rails at their present ingratitude after all he has done for them;[88] on another occasion he expresses surprise *(thaumazō)* that people seem only to remember the few harsh things he had to do and not the saving assistance he often rendered:

> But it is an honorable thing, surely, and just and holy and more pleasant to remember the good things rather than the bad.[89]

Only very gradually does the awareness grow in him that he cannot keep everything as perfect as he wants it and that his excellence does not insure permanence. He turns down the supreme command because he considers "that it is unclear to every man what the future will bring and therefore there is also a danger of losing the reputation one has already achieved."[90] He begins to think more and more of leaving the army and returning home to Athens. But he is always drawn back to the army in its need, even though he gets nothing for his efforts:

> Well, it is necessary, I suppose, for a man to expect everything when even I am now accused by you just when I

imagine to myself that I have exerted the greatest zeal on your behalf.⁹¹

The headstrong Xenophon who dropped everything to travel with Proxenos is not ignorant, let alone incompetent; he is merely too easily deceived, deceived about the nature and actions of others, deceived about his own nature and desires. He is his own worst enemy. As a seer tells him, even if money is about to come Xenophon's way, some obstacle will always appear, not the least being the obstacle he is to himself.⁹²

Xenophon's personality dominates most of the *Anabasis,* so clearly any attempt to explain the work must be made in terms of this. It cannot be forgotten, furthermore, that the record of the Ten Thousand Xenophon preserves is very much his own view. As Dürrbach pointed out in a classic study,⁹³ Diodoros' account makes no mention of Xenophon; and it is evident that Diodoros did not use the *Anabasis* as a source for events like Kounaxa. Since Xenophon published it under the pseudonym Themistogenes of Syracuse, he speaks of himself as a separate, different person, making it possible, as Plutarch long ago observed, to lend a greater air of verisimilitude to what he says about his own deeds.⁹⁴ It looks as though Xenophon had an apologetic purpose in mind, therefore, when he undertook the composition; and this may be what prompted Ephoros, Diodoros' source, to avoid it as a reliable record of what occurred on the march up-country.

Most commentary on the *Anabasis* has, in fact, been concerned with its alleged *Tendenz,* seeking explanations outside the work for those which it ought to contain within itself.⁹⁵ Why must Xenophon have necessarily had an immediately practical purpose in mind when writing the *Anabasis* or any other work? What was Xenophon writing an apology for? Was it a response to the account of the campaign written by one of his colleagues in command, Sophainetos? In the absence of significant portions of Sophainetos' work this must remain a gratuitous assumption.⁹⁶ Was it to respond to the charges made against him by others of the expedition or even to charges made against the men themselves by hostile Greeks in Asia Minor or in the fatherland? This, too, is unconvincing, for even if the earliest conceivable publication date is accepted, it remains obscure why Xenophon, at his ease in Skillous, waited more than a decade to defend himself or his army.[97] And even if it is assumed that he could have blown the dust off issues and events long past, why does he spend so much time in the *Anabasis* about so many things unrelated to *apologia*, like the character study of Cyrus, the different kinds of native dances, descriptions of foreign food and foreign customs, strategic devices like winter leggings, various kinds of bows, and ways to cut glare from the sunlit snow? What has *apologia* got to do with men chasing ostriches and wild donkeys or getting sick on honey? A work of defense, moreover, implies a certain method of operation by which evidence is sifted and selected for biased ends. Yet Xenophon seems free of such prejudice; he records both the folly and the heroism of the men prior to and after Kounaxa, he never displays partiality to one group over another, is content to call a man good or bad on his own personal merits, and, what is most important, his defenses of his own actions ultimately reveal his own folly.

To seek to explain the *Anabasis* in terms of a *Tendenz* is too narrow a view at best. The conflicts between Diodorus' source and Xenophon do not have to be explained by assuming that Xenophon had an ulterior motive which caused him to distort artfully what really happened. If Ephoros neglected Xenophon, it need not be the result of a superior historical understanding which led him to prefer Sophainetos, Ktesias, or whomever. Perhaps as a student of Isokrates he deliberately avoided the work of a known Socratic.[98] Or perhaps Ephoros found another account more suitable for his purposes, not because it was more accurate but because it was more straightforward, lacking all those details which give point and life to Xenophon's narrative. For the reader of Diodoros, even bearing in mind Diodoros is only providing a summary for inclusion within a much larger and different framework, would hardly get the idea that the march of the Ten Thousand was anything more than a series of military and geographical obstacles overcome.[99]

The *Anabasis*, to be sure, does record the actions of historical men in a definite time and place; but perhaps Xenophon never had historical precision uppermost in his mind as his chief aim. Thus even though he admits knowing Ktesias' account of Kounaxa, he does not follow it, despite the fact that Ktesias was closer to the center of action than Xenophon was.[100] Xenophon is more concerned with the heroic action of Cyrus, to show that his death was the sort to be expected from a man of his kind, to show that this death was indicative of the man's whole life. By the same token Xenophon may err in the geography of the army's route, but this is less an indication of Xenophon's sloppiness or his failure to consult even his own diaries (if they ever existed) than it is another indication that he was interested in something else which need not, moreover, have had anything to do with *apologia*. He records the numbers of stathmoi and parasangs traversed by the army of Cyrus not just to give his book an air of authenticity but to suggest quietly the ever deepening ensnarement of the Greeks within Persian territory. When the retreating force comes across some ruined cities of the Persian past, once again Xenophon records this not so much because the army did in reality pass by them but because they testify to the weakness of the Persians from whom the army is fleeing; for the ancient Persians conquered none of these places by force of arms but only owing to chance acts of nature.[101] Finally is it for accuracy's sake that Xenophon narrates how the Greeks, who thought they were home free once they had reached the sea, got sick on the local sweet, encountered in this region the most barbarian people they had ever seen, and found olives nonexistent amongst the regional produce?[102] Doubtless all these things happened, or things like them;[103] but within Xenophon's context they seem to have a resonance which transcends the purely reportorial, suggesting a truth about the army beyond its simple passage.

It would be better, therefore, to realize that the *Anabasis*, though dealing in a narrative and unfictionalized way with a historical event, is clearly one man's obviously idiosyncratic vision of that event, and that it was clearly meant to be understood as such. The *Anabasis* differs in its own angle of view from straightforward history, from the *Hellenika*, for example, just as the *Agesilaos* differs in its fashion.[104] Most simply put, the *Anabasis* records a young man's journey away from home and the experiences he had while traveling. But Xenophon also sees something more to it, that the desire to be away from his city was the desire of a personality infatuated with heroic champions like Cyrus who did not always observe the duties of custom and law and that the very life of travel he embarked upon for the chance to display his own *aretē* became a snare and a delusion when he blindly tried to effect something permanent. In this ability to preserve a perfect tension between the concrete events of a journey and the suggestion of a larger dimension behind them, the *Anabasis* recalls its ultimate literary forebear, the *Odyssey* of Homer; and Xenophon's explicit allusions to that poem perhaps best indicate his understanding of the nature of his own literary endeavor.[105]

Xenophon figures so much in the *Anabasis*, therefore, because it is about him and his life; it is avowedly, not deceitfully or apologetically, one-sided. But this prominence is also revealing, for it contrasts so markedly with Xenophon's retiring presence in most of his other works. It is in itself a further indication of that young spirit which went forth to seek its own fame and its own glory, which sought its own honor and failed to heed the voice of teacher or to respect the god.

The final remark of the *Anabasis* reports the arrival of Thibron and Xenophon's release from command, as the remnant of the Ten Thousand march against Tissaphernes.[106] What is on the mind of these men who before have thought only of Greece? What must that man have been thinking who imagined he would return to his fatherland stretched out like Odysseus? Doubtless the promises of pay and the new prospects for fortune and adventure make them forget. Fools that they are, they lose their day of homecoming.

Xenophon's own fate is similar. Desire as he may to leave the army, the gods will not permit it.[107] When eventually he returns to Greece, it is to a life in exile from Athens on an estate at Skillous. The god he tried to evade at Delphi has been vindicated. Even in his dream the night he rouses the army, he sees that there may be no escape:

> but on the other hand, because the dream came from Zeus the Great King and because the fire seemed to blaze in a circle, he was afraid lest he be unable to get out of the King's territory, but should be closed in on all sides by obstacles.[108]

How revealing it is, therefore, to find him so concerned at Skillous with the due observance of divine ritual and so aware of the danger of its neglect.[109] Even more revealing, however, is the simplicity and quiet of his life there. Family, farming, the hunt, it all seems somehow far removed from the adventures of an earlier day. He seems to have come to a new understanding about the nature of *philotimia*, the love of glory and fame, to have reduced the scope of his past ambitions to a contentment with place and the stability of the definite which he could not find while addicted to travel.

How far removed, as well, this is from Isokrates' panhellenic propaganda, with which the *Anabasis* is frequently associated. It is even thought that Isokrates in his *Panegyrikos* quotes from Xenophon, although the alleged echo is only of a common word, not a passage, and the context and character of the remarks differ one from the other.[110] There is no denying that the experience of the Ten Thousand soon became famous, and men of affairs both Greek and Persian often surmised what it boded for the future of barbarian and Hellenic conflict.[111] By 380 it is hardly surprising that a rhetorical pundit could see in it a living witness to the superiority of a united Hellas over the effete East, a rallying cry to rouse his countrymen from internal strife to a foreign holy war. But Xenophon knew more about Persia than most of his contemporaries and was only too well aware that its power was not easily toppled. As he himself put it, an intelligent observer recognized that the King's empire was strong in the extent of its territory and the number of its people, and weak only if attack was swift.[112] The *Anabasis* could not make more clear, either, how difficult leaving Persia could be and, more crucial still, how difficult and finally impossible it was to keep an army of Greeks united. It is not that Xenophon did not appreciate Persian weakness for what it was or that he did not harbor in his heart panhellenic hopes or desires. He may well have done so. But he seems to have known better than the vacuous nestorizings of Isokrates the difference between dream and reality.

For it is finally with this awareness that the *Anabasis* deals. Many have observed how misleading its title is; only the first book is a march up-country, the rest being a journey down to the sea. But perhaps the title itself indicates that literalism is a poor guide to the book's meaning and that misapprehension and deception are its recurring concerns. The *Anabasis* is not merely about a geographic ascent or the trick played by Cyrus on the Greeks. Rather it concerns the deeper deception many men play on themselves as they pursue what they think most important in life and what they think most gives it meaning, namely, *philotimia*, kingdom, power, and glory. Nothing better intimates a late date for the composition of the *Anabasis* than Xenophon's mature perception of this delusion, especially as it applies to himself, or the detachment with which he can examine his own actions as though he were writing about someone else, a certain "Xenophon" whom Themistogenes of Syracuse describes and who did not fully heed Socrates. But this also holds true for the Xenophon who lived at Skillous; for the life he led there was still deficient: it was not the life of a citizen of Athens. That is to say, the *Anabasis* may not have been possible until its author saw the contented peace of the estate shattered by Elean incursions, which compelled him to wander again. Perhaps he realized only when back in Athens, an exile no more, that only there could he genuinely pursue that quest to which Socrates might have continually invited him had he not foolishly gone after Cyrus:

> Οὐ μόνον ἐς Πέρσας ἀνέβη Ξενοφῶν διὰ Κῦρον,
> ἀλλ' ἄνοδον ζητῶν ἐς Διὸς ἥτις ἄγοι.
>
> Not only for Cyrus' sake did Xenophon march up towards the Persians
> But in search of a road which led up to Zeus.[113]

6
HISTORY

Mihi, quanto plura recentium seu veterum revolvo, tanto magis ludibria rerum mortalium cunctis in negotiis observantur.
— Tacitus

When Xenophon decided to write a history, it was inevitable that it would be a hellenica; local history was for narrower minds. Choice and chance had enabled him to travel widely and to live abroad from Athens so that he could know better than most of his contemporaries the nature of Persian cunning or the perverse intricacies of Peloponnesian politics. The necessity of exile could become for him the virtue it had been for Thucydides.

And of course it was as a continuation of Thucydides' unfinished work that Xenophon introduced his own with the abrupt and bold opening—"After these things." Unfortunately for Xenophon, however, this invitation to juxtapose the Hellenika and its great predecessor has only revealed for many the meagerness of Xenophon's historical awareness and the shoddiness of his historical method. As Grote put it, "to pass from Thucydides to the Hellenika of Xenophon is a descent truly mournful."[1] He omits too much, he condenses severely, especially in the first two books, and he seems over interested in the seemingly trivial to the neglect of the obviously important. More damning still was the criticism first voiced by Niebuhr[2] and repeated ever since (albeit less loudly)[3] that Xenophon's worth as an historian is cheapened further by his pronounced and unpatriotic Spartan bias: no Thucydidean objectivity here.

At the same time Niebuhr suggested that Xenophon might not have written the Hellenika during one continuous period, and he claimed that the work was a pastiche of Books One and Two plus Three through Seven. He did not base his belief on any statement of Xenophon intimating a new perception of events or mere interruptions in the time of writing (analogous to the so-called second preface of Thucydides) but on the concluding statement of the second book which reports the oath sworn in 401 by the reconciled Athenians after the tyrants have been expelled and the Eleusis slayings have taken place:

> And having sworn oaths that they would truly never remember grudges, still even now they carry on civic life together and the People abides by its oath.[4]

The time indication in this passage, "still even now," prompted Niebuhr to conclude that certain definite persons active in the late fifth century were not prosecuted for involvement with the Thirty Tyrants and that such trials would have been inconceivable more than, say, fifteen years after the oath-taking. But fifteen years is an arbitrary number, and it is really impossible to assign any exact time to these words. Furthermore a longer rather than a shorter time may be more correct, for the speeches of Lysias, especially the sixteenth, which is dated to 382, show that the memory of the Thirty in Athens lingered long.[5]

Niebuhr was only the first in a long line of critics of the *Hellenika* which continues to the present. His study was also symptomatic of what would develop later insofar as his theory about the time of composition was distinct from his views about the *Hellenika's* content. Thus, theories of the stages of its composition came forth as from a Pandora's box as quickly as writers could write; and from the original dichotomy there sprang a complex network of divisions whose interrelation was elaborated with an infinite variety of expertise. Help was also sought in statistics, for it seemed that Xenophon's use of particles could help to date the different sections of his work.[6]

The statistical argument was discredited as long ago as Schwartz, who made the common sense observation that Xenophon's narrative would determine his use of particles and that therefore their presence or absence betokened nothing for chronology.[7] A better understanding of Xenophon's Greek[8] and the discovery of new epigraphical evidence[9] aided in the reestablishment of a unitarian view. Finally two recent studies[10] have painstakingly reviewed the question and have convincingly revealed both the lapses in simple logic which afflict so much of the analytic approach and the failure of those who take it to base their arguments on an understanding of what Xenophon is trying to say in the *Hellenika* and what categories of thought he employs to structure his account. In the absence of new information to the contrary, it should be maintained that the *Hellenika* was written at one time, most likely in the mid-350s, since the latest event narrated occurred in 358 and Xenophon died around 354.[11]

Sad to say, the argument over the unity of the *Hellenika* has always tended to center on the time or times of its composition, not on its theme; and its relation to Thucydides' work has hardly been sufficiently examined to see if the connection is more than a simple chronological one, to see whether there may be something important in it despite those flaws of scientific technique for which nineteenth-century scholarship could never pardon it. The most important issues have been avoided. Even recently one scholar has wondered why Xenophon bothered to write history at all,[12] and another has suggested that his inability to keep the facts straight shows that he was an historical novelist, not an historian.[13]

But Xenophon was always aware of the requirements of the form in which he wrote, and if he had wanted to write fiction he would have made the *Hellenika* into another *Kyroupaideia*. Instructive as well is the contrast the parallel passages of the *Hellenika* and the *Agesilaos* present, which reveal Xenophon's conscious attempt in the former at a more restricted style and a content more inclusive and more objective. Gautier, who knew Xenophon's language as well as anybody, correctly stresses this point when he remarks that, though there may be differences of language in parts of the *Hellenika*, taken as a whole it clearly stands apart from the *Anabasis* or the *Kyroupaideia*.[14]

History has at least one basic requirement: it speaks of things which actually happened or were thought to have happened by actual people. What Xenophon speaks of in the *Hellenika* cannot be fiction, though it may be wrong or inadequate as far as facts are concerned. And because it speaks of things over and done, though actually experienced, it may seem less of an anomaly that Xenophon, so much of whose work is lived retrospective, set his hand to it. His act was deliberate, and his chosen opening made clear to what tradition of writing he wanted the *Hellenika* to belong. This is what is truly startling about it. For no other Socratic and no other philosopher before him had engaged in this activity,[15] and Plato seems unaware, perhaps intentionally, of Thucydides' masterpiece.[16] The most important questions about the *Hellenika*, therefore, concern not only what this means for the understanding of Xenophon's thought in itself, but also of the way in which he responded to the Thucydidean heritage of historiography.

It would be too facile to conclude that because the *Hellenika* shows throughout its length typical Xenophontic concerns (such as the nature of good and bad commanders), it is therefore not meant to be taken as Thucydidean.[17] The same can be said for viewing only the first two books (up to Athens' defeat and the destruction of its Long Walls) as uniquely Thucydidean, because this is where Thucydides meant to end his account and because only up to this point does Xenophon preserve the Thucydidean method of dating by summers and winters. There is, indeed, no reason to assume, even as a starting point, that Xenophon intended dutifully, if somewhat slavishly, merely to complete Thucydides;[18] both the Oxyrhynchos Historian and Theopompos wrote histories which began where Thucydides left off, but neither of them stopped at the end of the Peloponnesian War.

In fact, Xenophon's description of Athens' humiliation may provide a good place from which to begin a closer investigation of his manner and meaning. Lysander, he says, sailed into the Peiraieus, exiles returned home; and the walls were pulled down with gusto to the accompaniment of flutes, with everyone "thinking that this day would be the beginning of freedom for Greece."[19] No sooner has Xenophon written this than he immediately proceeds to list the various tyrannies which sprang up or were then active in the Greek world. Lykophron came to power in Pherai, where Jason would soon hold sway, and Dionysios was troubled in Syracuse. In Athens itself there were the Thirty, a group whose rise to prominence Xenophon puts in higher relief by omitting in his narrative certain events leading up to its appointment which might have detracted from the force gained by a straightforward linking with tyrannies elsewhere.[20] What Xenophon has done, in other words, is to insist consciously on a contrast which forces attention forward from his description of the jubilation over the War's conclusion in order to make clear that he himself does not share the narrative's confident sense of finality. It is one of the most basic assumptions underlying the Hellenika that history did not stop in 404 and that the Peloponnesian War directly influenced what happened subsequently in Greece. In this sense the opening words of the Hellenika, as well as its first two books, mark the work as retrospective not in the sense that it yearns nostalgically for the past but in the sense that present and past connect and that Greece in the fourth century cannot be understood without an appreciation of the trauma endured at the end of the fifth. Xenophon will conclude his history with a similar awareness:

> ἐμοὶ μὲν δὴ μέχρι τούτου γραφέσθω· τὰ δὲ μετὰ ταῦτα ἴσως ἄλλῳ μελήσει.
>
> Let this much be written by me; what happened after these things will, perhaps, be a concern to someone else.[21]

The flautists played a prelude, not a coda; but it introduces no era of peace and freedom, as Xenophon means to point up by juxtaposing the expectations of liberty with the reality of tyranny. He has undercut his own description with his customary perception of the difference between the appearance and the reality of things, and he also intimates that things do not always turn out as people expect them to. Moreover this perception is not limited to this one sequence of events; the entire Hellenika gives the lie to those aspirations of 404, for it is a history of repeated attempts at empire and the continual subversion of independence and order itself throughout the Greek world. The imperialistic trend set by Athens was continued by Sparta even as it proclaimed itself the liberator, and it was at Greek hegemony which Jason and Thebes also aimed. Only at Mantineia does Xenophon see a kind of culmination, for it was here, finally, that the bankruptcy of one kind of policy stood fully revealed and where Xenophon could most climactically display the irony of events:

> τούτων δὲ πραχθέντων τοὐναντίον ἐγεγένητο οὗ ἐνόμισαν πάντες ἄνθρωποι ἔσεσθαι.
>
> When these things were done, there had taken place just the opposite of what everyone thought would happen.[22]

This may also explain why Xenophon probably did not think of writing the *Hellenika* until Mantineia had enabled him to discover an interpretive framework for the events of his time such as Thucydides perceived he had ready-made from the beginning in the Peloponnesian War.

Mantineia is the culmination; it remains to discover how Xenophon shows the inevitable development to this point and to reveal the unified nature of his conception, which goes beyond the mere recurrence of familiar Xenophontic *topoi*. To consider first the opposition of thought and reality, of speech and action, it is necessary to distinguish among the deceits played upon an enemy in military campaigns, the deceits used to buoy up the spirits of a failing army, and the deceit used to cover up activity that is unmistakeably culpable or that would lack support if seen undisguised. The first two categories require little comment; examples come immediately to hand in the feints Agesilaos successfully employs against Tissaphernes or the trick Lysander plays upon the Athenians at Aigospotamoi.[23] Eteonikos tries to aid his army's morale by concealing the news of Arginousai, just as Agesilaos will not disclose to his army the news of Konon's victory at Knidos.[24] This last instance is especially noteworthy because Xenophon explicitly speaks of the power words have to get men to do what they might otherwise not do:

> Consequently when there was a skirmish against the enemy, Agesilaos' men won owing to the report that the Spartans were victorious in the sea battle.[25]

It may be wondered, however, whether Xenophon thinks men always recognize when deceit is permissible and when it is not. He may, in fact, suggest that the very atmosphere of war is conducive to the blurring of necessary distinctions. For example Agesilaos is quick to fault Tissaphernes for his mendacity in violating a sacred oath,[26] but he himself is not averse to lying to his fellow Spartans when he needs to save face. When the Theban Kadmeia has been lost, he declines to lead an expedition to regain it, pleading the excuse of age. But his real reason, Xenophon says, is his fear of being accused of troubling Sparta in order to aid in the restoration of tyrants.[27]

Agesilaos is not the only Spartan with a gift for concealing the unpalatable or whose words do not coincide with his thoughts or deeds. Kallikratidas at Methymna proclaims that he will never enslave Greeks, only to put up for sale some captive Athenians.[28] Lysander, the victor at Aigospotamoi, holds a council to debate the fate of the Athenians he has captured. The allies vote the death penalty whereupon Lysander asks one of the generals under sentence, Philokles, "what he thought a man should suffer who had started the violation of Greeks' rights?"[29] (Philokles has had thrown overboard the crews of two captured enemy ships.) Lysander gives him no time to reply, but slits his throat, doubtless meaning to seem a man passionately devoted to Greek liberty. But in what way is Lysander's meting out of death to a beaten enemy any more impartial than Philokles' has been? It must also be noted, as Xenophon observes, that one Athenian, Adeimantus, is let free. Xenophon leaves it in doubt whether this is because he has opposed the maiming of defeated foes or because he has betrayed the fleet to Lysander and the Spartan allies;[30] but there can be no doubt about the version Lysander preferred, who was intelligent enough to appreciate the public value of what looked like justice.

Lysander, of course, was also responsible for the imposition of harmosts and decarchies on Greek cities to insure their subservience, not to mention his installing the Thirty in Athens. This betrayal of the liberty for which Sparta has supposedly led the Greeks against Athens is one cause of the Corinthian War. The Thebans, in appealing to Athens to join in the conflict, can claim that the Spartans have deceived their fellow Hellenes and that instead of providing freedom they have provided a slavery twice as bad as that before.[31] Also on the minds of the Thebans is the Spartan campaign against the Eleans, which the Spartans have advertised as a war to secure autonomy for the neighboring cities of Elis but which Xenophon himself shows is the result of old grudges.[32]

Autonomy, in fact, becomes the central word in the *Hellenika's* investigation of the abuse of speech and its dissociation from reality. Agesilaos goes to Asia Minor ostensibly to secure the freedom of Greek cities from Persia,[33] but his decision to leave Greece at Aulis in the manner of Agamemnon rightly causes the Thebans alarm about his sense of his own position.[34] By the same token, when he is recalled to Greece, he travels "by the same road which the Great King took when he warred against Hellas."[35] In the *Agesilaos* Xenophon makes a similar statement, but as an encomiastic friend he adds that the Spartan completed the same distance as Xerxes in less than a month.[36] Xenophon the historian deletes the praise and leaves an ominous parallel.

Once Sparta has secured its stewardship of the Peace of Antalkidas, which includes guarantees of autonomy and freedom, it does not hesitate to apply sanctions selectively and to further thereby its own self-aggrandizement. Thus the Theban Confederacy is dissolved, as well as the union of Corinth and Argos. Akanthian autonomy provides a propaganda screen for Sparta to increase its power in the north against the Olynthian federation, a campaign Sparta's allies encourage because they want to please the Lacedaemonians.[37] Sparta forces the dissolution of federations wherever they seem to threaten Spartan power, not to obtain autonomy for smaller and down-trodden cities; and needless to say it preserves federations when expedient, as when Achaia and Kalydon unite during the Corinthian War.[38] The lesson of Mantineia, compelled to split into separate villages by a Spartan army which used the city's own river to undermine its fortifications, is not one in political justice or freedom, but rather, as Xenophon wryly observes, in urban design: a city should not let a river run through its walls.[39]

Sparta's attempts to obtain greater and greater power climax with Phoibidas' seizure of the Theban Kadmeia at the behest of the oligarchical party, whose usurpation of the city's government he then protects. He has acted on his own initiative and against orders, but he is not punished. Agesilaos argues that it would be just to punish Phoibidas if he has done something harmful to his city; in fact he has done it a favor.[40] Not justice, utility; it was the Spartan program in a nutshell. Agesilaos also arranges for the acquittal of Sphodrias, although he too has acted rashly and indeed so enraged the Athenians by an attempted assault on the Peiraieus that they will soon ally again with Thebes, with the Spartan disaster at Leuktra the ultimate outcome. But Sphodrias is a man who has always been honorable before, "and it was difficult to kill this sort of man. Sparta had need of such soldiers."[41]

When Sparta's enterprises have failed and the city seeks alliance with Athens, its leaders have to listen to a forceful indictment by the Athenian ambassador Autokles:

> And furthermore what is diametrically opposed to autonomy you establish, here rules of ten, there rules of thirty; and when these are in control you take care, not that they rule legally, but that they can control the cities by force. And so you seem pleased more by tyrannies than by constitutional government.[42]

Autokles, impolitic as he may be, speaks bluntly and to the point. He not only exposes the falsehoods behind the Spartans' operations, as he brings out the conflict between what Sparta has said and what it has done; more important, he suggests that imperialism ultimately is tyranny based upon the desire to have more, *pleonexia*.[43] This holds true, it must be stressed, both for the actions of Lysander and for the deeds of less flamboyant or more typically conservative Spartans like Agis or Agesilaos; Xenophon sees a consistent aim in Spartan policy which the opposition of men like Pausanias or Antalkidas could not alter. He also sees how Sparta's aggressive attitude works its own undoing. For it immediately provokes the hostility of powers which finally Sparta can not overcome militarily; and, more profoundly, it abets the violation of internal Spartan customs whose subversion only vilifies the city further in the eyes of others and encourages their disaffection.

Autokles is concerned only with Sparta, but he actually sums up the imperialist temper of his time. Self-aggrandizement, imperialism, and tyranny constantly recur in the *Hellenika* as a nexus involving self-serving deceit, violence, and the disruption of civil polity, including that of the power-seeking cities themselves. It would appear, in other words, that Xenophon observes in his view of history that *poleis* acting individually do not always act from motives radically different from those of individual citizens. He confronts here precisely those features of existence which he has elsewhere examined in more limited settings, although he remains most attentive still to the deeds of various individual leaders to follow the vagaries of their cities' fortunes. Patriotism, as de Tocqueville observes, is many times just the extension of individual selfishness.[44]

Thus the Athenian tyrant Kritias can confess outright that it is impossible for those who want more for themselves *(tois pleonektein boulomenois)*[45] not to remove any who stand in their way. This same Kritias also expresses the highest praise for Sparta in the *Hellenika*. Arguing against the scruples of Theramenes and insisting on the need for total allegiance to the ruling clique, he proclaims:

> The best form of government certainly seems to be the Spartan. If one of the ephors there should try to fault the government and to oppose what is being done instead of obeying the majority, do you not think he would be deemed by the ephors themselves and the entire rest of the city to be worthy of the greatest punishment?[46]

Sparta's policy of aggression ultimately brings it low, and the tyranny of the Thirty follows the same pattern. Their program of murder for profit and their confiscation of wealth and private arms alienate many, who eventually return from flight to restore the democracy. The tyrants in Athens even violate their own laws when they convict and execute Theramenes.[47] His death is an object lesson in the frustration which Xenophon sees at the heart of tyranny. Xenophon admires Theramenes' toast to Kritias with the fatal hemlock, but doubt must remain about his admiration for Theramenes' life. Too many of Kritias' accusations against him ring true, especially about his role in the prosecution of the generals after Arginousai. Theramenes' own reply catches him in a lie, as his justification conflicts with Xenophon's narrative of that sordid affair;[48] and even what he openly admits in his own defense may well cause wonder whether the best interests of Athens were ever his concern when he concluded a peace with Sparta. He opposed seizure of citizen weapons only because he thought the Spartans did not want a weak Athens, incapable of helping them in their endeavors.[49] In fact considered simply as speeches, both the attack of Kritias and the defense of Theramenes have much in common; each brings forth the usual rhetorical devices, returns smear for smear, and finally shows that each is more like than unlike the other.[50] The irony of Theramenes' final joke, then, is two-fold; by his insistence on humor he manages to assert the very freedom the tyrants have sought to deny him and others, thus triumphing even in his defeat. But there is also the awareness that he has fallen victim to the very system he himself has helped engineer.

The career of Euphron, the petty tyrant of Sikyon, provides a parallel, for he changes sides the way Theramenes was said to change boots. Alternating with breath-taking ease and expedience between democratic and oligarchic policies, his aim is simple: power for himself.[51] As a typical tyrant he kills or banishes opponents, seizes property, including temple revenues, and engages in deceit to save face.[52] When making excuses to the Spartans, he can even make bold to claim that he has been their friend all along; but, as Xenophon points out, though many heard him it was not very clear how many believed him.[53] And like other tyrants Euphron dies violently, assassinated at a conference in Thebes; and his assassin is exonerated.[54] Euphron can hardly be considered a major figure of Greek history, but Xenophon includes him in the *Hellenika* as an instance, minor though not therefore unimportant, of the operation of tyranny and the havoc it wreaks. For the tyrant of Sikyon, in pursuing personal ambition, only serves to confuse and disrupt further the relations of the men and cities around him. Tyranny by definition is a government based more upon whim than legality; its working out of its ambitions must therefore inevitably effect more unrest than stability, an unrest which, however, ultimately destroys its own promoter.

Euphron's assassination, even though its particular timing comes as a surprise, is something that ought not to be unexpected; the actions of tyrants induce others to imitate their own ruthlessness. Much the same can be said for the most cunning tyrant of all, Jason of Pherai, who also dies as an assassin's victim and not, it would seem superficially considered, as a necessary victim of his own programs. Indeed, his fortunes seem at their height when he falls,[55] and he is a man who has every reason to think he will succeed. Xenophon describes him in the speech of Polydamas, a Pharsalian whose city is threatened by Pheraian expansion. He is said to be a man robust in body and mind, in absolute control of his physical and mental capacities, and who is always able to obtain full service from his army.[56] He shares, in other words, many of the qualities the typical Xenophontic hero possesses,[57] and Xenophon goes so far as to call him the greatest man of his time in view of his power and prestige.[58] But his aim is his own advancement, not peace in Greece, let alone the pursuit of virtue. After Leuktra he plays Thebes and Sparta off against one another in a game that had gone on since the Persians entered into the last phase of the Peloponnesian War, all the while assuring each city of his simple concern for its well-being.[59] The very danger of Jason, in other words, is that he possesses, as it were, all the virtues, but is still immoral. Xenophon does not explain the motives of his slayers, but the fact that they are welcomed almost everywhere in Greece as men who have removed a tyrant[60] suggests that tyranny will inevitably invite assaults from those in search of honor or liberty, or from those who are likewise in search of power for themselves.

Nonetheless, as inevitable in one sense as Jason's death is, there is little necessity for it to have happened when it did, and Xenophon is at pains to emphasize Jason's radical change of fortune by building up the image of his power just before the fatal blow falls. But this is only one example of the *Hellenika's* pervasive interest in the mutability of human events and their frequent unexpectedness. Beginning with his narration of the final years of the Peloponnesian War, Xenophon shows how all too frequently plans are upset, often with disastrous consequences. Kallikratidas, the Spartan admiral who means to stop Konon from fornicating the sea, is himself drowned in the defeat at Arginousai.[61] Alkibiades is dismissed after the defeat at Notion for which, not he, but a disobedient subordinate, is responsible.[62] One defeat and he is out, the darling of the People now its scorned, even after he has managed a successful return to Athens and has effected the militarily and politically clever ploy of carrying on the Mysteries' procession by land instead of by sea.[63] The Syracusan Hermokrates, whose abilities Xenophon expatiates upon, is forced into an exile, whose suddeness Xenophon emphasizes by narrating it just after he has described how amicably Hermokrates' contingent fares with the Antandrians and how this leader appreciates Tissaphernes' double game with Persian gold.[64]

During the Corinthian War, as well, unexpected peripeties abound. Not reluctant to fight the Thebans, the Spartans, Xenophon reports, are only looking for an excuse to settle old scores and to put an end to their enemy's insolence *(pausai tēs . . . hubreōs)*.[65] But this confident expectation will not be realized; the battle at Haliartos will end with Lysander dead and King Pausanias retreating with a Spartan army which the Boiotians assail "quite insolently" *(mala hubristikōs)*.[66] Reversals also beset Agesilaos. After success in Thessaly and news of a Spartan victory at Nemea, he is informed of the sea disaster Konon effected at Knidos.[67] And Xenophon stresses the force of this reversal by narrating

Konon's victory out of sequence, since it more naturally ought to be included in the otherwise unified account of naval operations which occurs *en bloc* at the end of Book Four. Xenophon emphasizes the famous defeat of the Spartan *mora* at Lechaion by first recounting how the Spartan hoplites have mocked their allies' fear of Iphikrates' peltasts as a childish fear of the bogeyman.[68] It is clear that he has bothered to report this incident at all only to be able better to reveal the shock of defeat to their confidence. Finally, Sparta's campaigns against Olynthos in the name of the Peace of the Antalkidas build from one success to another (including the serendipity of Phoibidas' seizure of the Kadmeia), only to be marred by the death of that most able Lacedaemonian leader, Teleutias.[69]

Reversals such as these should not, however, be thought always inexplicable because unexpected. Agesilaos is in a way responsible for the defeat of Sparta at Knidos, which catches him by surprise, for he himself appointed his brother-in-law Peisandros to command the Spartan fleet, even though Peisandros had no experience of naval affairs.[70] Justified once again, therefore, is the complaint of Sparta's allies during the Peloponnesian War that they got men like Kallikratidas when someone like Lysander was obviously more capable.[71] But Agesilaos always looked after his own. He favors the aquittal of Sphodrias perhaps out of a desire to please his son, the lover of Sphodrias' son;[72] and he can even attempt to "fix" the Olympic Games for a friend.[73] The gratifications of friendship do not, therefore, always recommend themselves as the inspiring principles of political and military action. They can lead to bizarre, not to say, comical, disadvantage. During the Corinthian War part of the Athenian fleet, financed by the Persian King, goes to aid Evagoras, a friend of the city but an enemy of Persia, only to be intercepted by the Spartans who, though hostile to Persia, thereby help the King to suppress one of his rebels. Both Athens and Sparta, Xenophon remarks, acted directly contrary to their own interests.[74]

The Spartans' entry into the Corinthian War also reveals how passion may subvert all the logic in the world.[75] They reckon that there is no better time to commence hostilities, but their motive is anger of long standing *(palai orgizomenoi)*, just as earlier this same anger prompted them to move against Elis.[76] In the same way, they punished Pausanias with the death penalty for his reasonable decision to retreat from Haliartos after gathering his dead under truce,[77] because he refused to be foolishly heroic—and because he aided the Athenian democrats at the time of the Thirty.[78]

Equally important is the role of passions in the decisions of individual men. Teleutias, whom Xenophon praises for his noble qualities, nonetheless succumbs to rage *(orgistheis)* at the sight of Olynthian cavalry cutting down his own men. He rushes into battle with his "phalanx in confusion," only to meet his death.[79] Mental confusion, mirrored in tactical disorder, has prevented control. When this can happen to a man of Teleutias' calibre, it is not surprising that men of lesser stature are easily overcome. So Phoibidas, before his assault on the Kadmeia which would have so many repercussions, is described as a man who is neither logical *(logistikos)* nor careful *(phronimos)* but who becomes light-headed at any thought of a glorious exploit, since he prefers glory to life itself.[80] Self-conceit may be behind the Athenian generals' dismissal of Alkibiades when he comes to warn them about the dangers of their position prior to the battle at Aigospotamoi. They tell him to go away, Xenophon says, because *they*, not he, are in command.[81] When during the 360s Lykomedes mouths the rhetoric of Arcadian nationalism, his hearers are "puffed up" with a sense of their own grandeur, so that they love him exceedingly and think he alone is a man.[82] Yet Lykomedes' devices are more than a little responsible for the contemporary chaos of the Peloponnesos and the antagonisms which finally cost him his life.[83]

One reversal and its causes require separate treatment, the battle of Arginousai and its aftermath. This victory, achieved against such incredible odds, is ruined by the prosecution of the generals for their failure to rescue the shipwrecked. Popular politicians in a rampant democracy lose all sense and factionalism carries the day but loses an empire. The generals delegated the task of picking up survivors to others, among them Theramenes, but when a chance storm prevents the rescue, the generals do not seek to pass the blame to them:

> "And not just because they accuse us," they said, "will we speak falsely, saying that those men are to blame; but we say that the size of the storm is what prevented the rescue."[84]

Eyewitnesses corroborate their testimony, and it seems as if the generals will be freed; but Theramenes, ever fearful for his own position, resorts to the cheapest sort of tricks to keep public opinion turned against his former commanders. At the festival of families, the Apatouria, the moaning of people pretending to be kinsmen of those lost, along with the well-timed appearance of a man who has made it to safety by floating on a barrel and who reports the alleged curses of comrades drowning around him, bring about the condemnation Theramenes desires.[85] The final appeal made by Euryptolemos on behalf of the generals is a moving one whose precise antitheses are an appeal and a witness to the very logic which the People would ignore:

> μὴ τοίνυν, ὦ ἄνδρες Ἀθηναῖοι, ἀντὶ μὲν τῆς νίκης καὶ τῆς εὐτυχίας ὅμοια ποιήσητε τοῖς ἡττημένοις τε καὶ ἀτυχοῦσιν, ἀντὶ δὲ τῶν ἐκ θεοῦ ἀναγκαίων ἀγνωμονεῖν δόξητε, προδοσίαν καταγνόντες ἀντὶ τῆς ἀδυναμίας.

> So then men of Athens, do not, in return for victory and good fortune, act like men vanquished and unfortunate, do not, in return for the ineluctable acts of god, appear harsh and condemn these men for treachery in the face of their powerlessness.[86]

The trial of the generals is not, however, only an example of mental blindness caused by ultimately stupid and self-serving men who can successfully arouse mass emotion. Xenophon also wants to make clear that the trial is illegal. The generals at the first hearing are not allowed to speak as long as the law permits, and at their last hearing they are illegally tried and condemned as a group. Only Socrates, a member of the presiding committee, refuses to move the charge, since he will do nothing against the law, while the crowd shouts that it is intolerable if it can not do what it wants.[87]

The mob has, in a sense, tyrannized, and in the process it

reveals that its failure to control itself lies behind its failure to control its military activities and its imperial diplomacy. Aigospotamoi is inevitable but superfluous; Sparta wins its hegemony by default. So Athens suffers the ultimate reversal as its citizens, on that night when no one sleeps, think they will suffer just what they have inflicted on the Melians, Histiaians, Skioneans, Toronians, and other Greeks;[88] and they reckon later, in the extremities of siege, that there is no saving themselves from the wrongs they have done to small cities, not in order to take understandable vengeance but to satisfy their arrogance, and for no other reason than because these cities have fought together with the other side.[89]

The example of imperial Athens brought low because of its own deeds and to its own surprise stands as a paradigm for the mistakes of other individuals, cities and men, with imperial ambitions in the fourth century. It was the misfortune of Greece in that time to fail to learn Athens' lesson. The Peloponnesian War left a counterfeit legacy of further entanglements; it had really settled nothing. Athens, Sparta, Jason, and Euphron all fit a similar pattern of self-advancement which becomes self-destruction as justice is violated in the quest for more and more power. Athens was untrue to its own principles of democratic freedom at home and overseas, while Sparta clearly promoted favorable tyrannies and violated its own code in incidents like the acquittal of Sphodrias, which Xenophon calls the most unjust verdict ever given in a Spartan court.[90]

Indeed Xenophon suggests that Sparta was never meant for imperial status in the first place or for the role of overseer of Greek autonomy. No sooner has Thibron gone abroad to free the Ionians than he alienates the very people he is supposed to help,[91] while his more capable successor Derkylidas pursues his own personal satisfactions, settling an old grudge against Pharnabazos when Tissaphernes is the ostensible foe[92] and making jokes about justice with the hapless blackguard Meidias.[93] More revealing still is the conspiracy in Sparta itself headed by Kinadon, a man who resents his exclusion from the Spartan elite corps.[94] When he is found out and arrested, the authorities ask him why he wants a revolution. "I did not want," he replies, "to be the inferior of anyone in Lacedaemon."[95] His answer and his execution after he is led around the city with his hands and neck bound in a dog collar *(kloios)*[96] must prompt the question how Sparta can proclaim itself the protector of equality and autonomy for the Greek world, when it does not practice real freedom at home. As if to reinforce this point, Xenophon also reports how Thrasyboulos, leader of the restored democracy of Athens, asks those who supported the Spartan-backed Thirty whether they had confidence in their actions because the Spartans were their allies:

> πῶς, οἵγε ὥσπερ τοὺς δάκνοντας κύνας κλοιῷ δήσαντες παραδιδόασιν, οὕτω κἀκεῖνοι ὑμᾶς παραδόντες τῷ ἠδικημένῳ τούτῳ δήμῳ οἴχονται ἀπιόντες;
>
> How so? For they, like men who hand over a biting dog after they have muzzled it, hand you over to the People you wronged and then leave you in the lurch.[97]

Sparta like Athens failed as an imperial power. Finally there were Thebes and Epameinondas. The Thebans throughout the *Hellenika*, be they democrats or oligarchs, appear as men no less interested in power than others. They oppose Spartan actions against the army of Thrasyboulos in Athens and against the Eleans, not because they are against aggression, but because they are against any increase in Sparta's strength. The same principle guides their disruption of Agesilaos' sacrifice in the manner of Agamemnon at Aulis and their appeal for assistance in the Corinthian conflict to the very Athens they had wanted obliterated in 404. They are quick to talk about justice, but their appeals are no less self-serving than those of the Spartans.[98] When they try to explain their former hostility to Athens, they even suggest that it was not the considered action of the city but only of an individual citizen who just happened to be at the deliberations over the fate of the defeated foe and who favored harsh measures.[99] Exculpation once again invites mendacity. Kangaroo courts are also evident at Thebes as they are elsewhere; thus Ismenias the democrat is executed following a trial rigged by his oligarchical enemies whom the Spartans on the Kadmeia protect.[100] And like any good guarantor of

Greek autonomy, Pelopidas makes a journey to the king of Persia; but Thebes' aim is always hegemony and self-advancement *(pleonexia)*.[101]

On the other hand, the Thebans are no fools. After their great victory at Leuktra, they are not led astray by their own success into risky action when invading the Peloponnesos; they keep their discipline and are generally able to capitalize on their enemies' mistakes.[102] Their great general Epameinondas is first introduced as a man who knows how to obtain friends and keep them, for he makes it a point not to change the internal constitutions of needed allies.[103] His campaign leading up to Mantineia is one which Xenophon says cannot be criticized for its forethought and daring, and he praises outright a number of the Theban's individual operations.[104] Above all he admires Epameinondas' virtues as a commander of men who could maintain an army which tired at no labor by day or by night, which shirked no danger, and which still desired to obey though short of supplies.[105] Xenophon especially marvels at this particular ability because Epameinondas' campaign is not prospering. He has incurred a defeat at the hands of an Athenian cavalry contingent, and his invasion of the Peloponnesos has effected a coalition, including Athens and Sparta, against him.[106] Thebes has also been quite unable to control the factions of that region to its own advantage, while the Thebans themselves sometimes work against one another, for Epameinondas' superiority does not go unchallenged at home.[107] In spite of all this Epameinondas is able to keep his head and hold his army in order. He deliberates; he does not act in haste or out of passion:

> Consequently, it seemed impossible to him to depart without a fight, since he reckoned that if he won he could make good all his mistakes. And if he should die, he considered his would be an honorable end since he was trying to leave dominion of the Peloponnesos to his fatherland.[108]

Die he does at Mantineia, and as a result Thebes cannot follow up on its victory. The individual's quest for glory and the city's end together.[109] No one is left in control, much to everyone's surprise, and Xenophon is moved to describe, in compelling and eloquent language, the confusion which makes Greece worse off than it was before. But Xenophon may not have found the outcome as astonishing as his contemporaries, for the irresolution of 362 is, in fact, the expression of the self-deceit and self-destruction of an age. Mantineia is the necessary outcome, in one sense, of the policies pursued earlier by leaders in Athens, then in Sparta and Thebes, not to mention Jason and Euphron. Paradoxically the attempts by competing powers to obtain undisputed hegemony weaken them internally, cost them many of their best men, and leave Greece without direction. States and their leaders, as Xenophon emphasizes in the case of Epameinondas, have acted, ultimately, out of a desire for honor and glory, prestige before the eyes of the world no matter the price. Greek cities and Greek men that they are, they are addicted to *philotimia*.[110] Xenophon has always known in the *Hellenika* where one kind of policy leads, and Mantineia is its historical upshot.

But there is a sense in which Mantineia is more profoundly unsettling and which makes Xenophon's statement about the unexpectedness of its outcome all the more disturbing. For while his history examines the consequences of certain developments, it would not be unreasonable to speculate that Greece would have been different if Epameinondas had lived. Epameinondas considered the possibility of his death, for it was one of the risks of battle; but nowhere does Xenophon indicate he thought about its effect on Thebes and the Theban hegemony. Xenophon has been at pains in the *Hellenika* to investigate why men and programs fail, and he makes it clear that often the answer is passion of one sort or another which obstructs clear thought. But Epameinondas is never portrayed with these failings. For all his mental abilities, something escaped his notice; he did not foresee the real implications of his dying. And by the same token there was nothing necessary about this death at Mantineia, for he might just as well have survived; and his superior generalship, in fact, made this outcome the more likely.

Xenophon does not mention Epameinondas by name until late in the *Hellenika* and even lets his responsibility for the great victory at Leuktra go unnoticed. It has often been argued that Xenophon's Spartan bias causes him to suppress as much mention of the Theban leader as he can, but it may be questioned whether such a bias exists at all; and in any event the indisputable praise Epameinondas receives when he does appear sufficiently rebuts this assessment of Xenophon's presentation.[111] Rather it may be that he is saved to the end to make the final reversal of the *Hellenika* all the more shattering in its climax. For Epameinondas is not lucky, *eutukhēs*, in spite of all his planning.[112] Though death in a battle may be expected at one time or another by a man zealous for honor and fame, why is it at this particular battle, where so much hinges upon his survival, that he falls mortally wounded?

Xenophon can give no answer to this question save to say that god brought it about that both sides at Mantineia gathered their dead under truce and found themselves at a loss about what further to do. Xenophon elsewhere in his account has also found some things ultimately inexplicable and often associates them with divinity. The storm at Arginousai no one could have forecast, let alone its consequences for the Athenian generals. The courage of the Eleans in a conflict around Olympia prompts Xenophon to remark that the gods can inspire in a day the kind of exploits it would take men a very long time to elicit from troops not naturally brave in the first place.[113] The folly of the Spartans, who against all sensible advice directed the hapless Kleombrotos to the disaster at Leuktra, can only move Xenophon to remark that they must have been impelled by some more-than-human power; no rational understanding is possible.[114] Indeed the entire reversal of Sparta's fortunes at the time of its ouster from Thebes can be seen, Xenophon says, as one example among many in the Greek and Persian world of how the gods are mindful of those who are sacrilegious and irreverent.[115] But Xenophon does not mean to imply that the gods are celestial puppeteers pulling the strings of historical causality; they merely represent the way things are. The world in which men live and act is neither fully explicable nor totally inexplicable. Reason and folly, the expected and the unforeseen, exist side by side; the why and wherefore of everything eludes the mind as well as it illumines it. As Xenophon puts it in an important but overlooked passage about a battle between the Spartans and Epameinondas:

> As for what happened next, it is possible to say that the gods were responsible, and it is also possible to say that no one could resist men so beside themselves.[116]

Thus Mantineia is the inevitable culmination of the *Hellenika* in more than one way. It was on this battlefield that Xenophon saw both the comprehensible working out of conflicting imperial desires with their attendant costly follies, and the yet hard-to-fathom reversals which can so profoundly disturb human action. Seen in this light the entire history comes back upon itself; for Xenophon begins his work in the midst of events, as it were, with no formal preface, and he ends it in a similarly open fashion with no firm conclusion reached and only the statement that perhaps someone else would narrate what happened "after these things." There is a sense here of history's sameness deep down, that the past will inevitably contain the future, that men's nature is constant and their ability to control passion or to understand what they do imperfect. If men could know everything, they would cease to be men and would become like the gods.

The complexity of Xenophon's awareness in the *Hellenika*, so rarely appreciated, will also explain why he nowhere betrays within its pages any simplistic faith in the ability of cities or individuals to overcome the inherent temptations of power. He must have agreed with the words of a northern Greek who in speaking to none other than the Spartans avers:

> For god has perhaps so arranged human affairs that the proud designs of men increase as power increases.[117]

There is no doubt that Xenophon admired the simple virtues where he saw them, and in the *Hellenika* he will even go out of his way to praise them. He will describe, for instance, the honesty and trustworthiness of the Pharsalian Polydamas, who introduces the Spartans to the menace of the self-seeking Jason and whose own life shows up Jason's for the fraud it is.[118] Likewise Xenophon digresses at some length to recount the loyalty and nobility of the Phleiasians;[119] for they possess that one quality, fidelity to their word, whose lack helps bring on chaos in Greece and enables the shiftiness of someone like Euphron to flourish. Yet Xenophon by no means implies that such fidelity can always be a safe guide to correct action in a less-than-perfect world.

This Phleiasian loyalty to Sparta should always be remembered, for instance, in the speeches of Prokles, a Phleiasian diplomat who is also the guest-friend of Agesilaos. He delivers two addresses in the *Hellenika*, both ardent appeals to the Athenians for their aid to Lacedaemon against Thebes. The first, while it displays some awareness of the realities of the situation—the danger for Athens as well as Sparta of a too-powerful Thebes in the wake of Leuktra—[120] is all too ready to suggest alliance on the basis of ancient history and old traditions. Prokles can even state that the Athenians could have no better defenders on land than the Spartans, who had given their utmost at Thermopylai.[121] He has conveniently forgotten Leuktra. He seems convinced as well that giving help to a city in need will insure absolutely its undying gratitude, although the relations of Athens and Thebes hardly bear him out. And this loyal Phleiasian is all too certain that the eyes of gods and men, Greek and barbarian, seeing all that happens, will prevent the Spartans from ever acting basely to Athens, if it brings them help in adversity.[122] In his second speech he also sees the hand of god at work in Athens' naval superiority and Sparta's preeminence in land warfare.[123] Thus he recommends an allied force commanded by Athens on the sea and Lacedaemon on the continent.[124] But once again his appeals for Sparta's interest do not square with the facts of Xenophon's own narrative, which has shown the Spartans defeated on land by the Athenian Iphikrates, not to mention the Leuktra debacle.[125] It has all too readily been assumed that Prokles' ideas are Xenophon's, since Xenophon was anti-Theban and pro-Spartan. But it should by now be apparent that this is facile in the extreme and that while Prokles, faithful to a fantasy, may have favored an Athens-Sparta alliance recalling the policy allegedly developed by Kimon in another age,[126] Xenophon need not have. Xenophon the historian is only too aware of the justice of Athenian complaints that the Spartans say one thing when disadvantaged but act quite differently when prospering.[127]

A kind of historical blindness similar to Prokles' can also be discerned in the speech of the conceited Athenian Kallias at the important congress in Sparta just prior to Leuktra. Kallias is a man aware of his own and his family's role in diplomatic affairs, but he has little practical sense of what is what. So he can say that it was never right for the Athenians and the Spartans to have gone to war because the first foreigners to whom the ancient Athenians revealed the Mysteries were Lacedaemonians and it was to them that Athens first gave the seed of Demeter's grain.[128] This can hardly be taken as a rigorous and astute response to the situation Xenophon has described in the *Hellenika*, and the blunt and forceful words of the next speaker, Autokles, point up their fatuity. Men like Prokles and Kallias are not the only ones of their time to live in a dream of the past—and not for nothing have parallels been noted between their statements and the orations of Isokrates.[129] Isokrates, Prokles, and Kallias might discourse at length about the glories of a heroic age and the halcyon era of Marathon and Salamis, but Xenophon knew better, because he had appreciated more fully the implications of the Peloponnesian War as well as the realities of human nature.

There are in the *Hellenika*, however, at least two men of affairs whose speeches Xenophon may be said to approve, Kallistratos of Aphidna and Thrasyboulos. Speaking in reply to Kallias and Autokles, Kallistratos' remarks reveal an awareness of the real facts missing in Kallias' and the understanding not shared by Autokles that righteous indignation is ruinous if it remains unbending. So he can say that both Athens and Sparta have made mistakes, and because they have both suffered for them, they can the more easily deal with one another.[130] He is aware of the aims of the Persian king, and he also knows that enlightened self-interest is what motivates sensible diplomacy. "I do not admire," he says, "the gambling man who doubles his wager after an initially lucky success; for most people of that sort end up losing everything."[131] It is worthwhile to note as well that Kallistratos nowhere in his speech mentions the gods Prokles so often invokes. He learns his lessons from the facts as he sees them, and his fundamental assessment is also one of the principal insights of the *Hellenika*:

> Therefore I now hope that we who have learned that self-aggrandizement *(to pleonektein)* is profitless will once again be moderate in our friendship with one another.[132]

Moderation and contentment with what is one's own are also ideas prominent in the words of Thrasyboulos to the reconciled oligarchs in Athens. He asks them why they tried to lord it over their fellow citizens, and he proceeds to demonstrate to them that they can make no sensible or justifiable claim to superiority. In fact their calculations of power and support, and especially their reliance on Sparta, have all proved incorrect. What is required is not confusion *(tarattesthai)* but adherence to the established laws of Athens.[133] With law comes justice, peace, and order; and this finally explains the import of Xenophon's words which Niebuhr apparently mistook. The fact that the Athenian People "still even now" carry on civic life together and abide by its oaths is meant not as an off-hand comment indicating a specific period of time but as an enduring praise for a polity which alone remains basically true to itself and its form of government in the topsy-turvy world of fourth-century Greece. The Athenians have taken to heart the first advice Thrasyboulos gives them:

> Ὑμῖν, ἔφη, ὦ ἐκ τοῦ ἄστεως ἄνδρες, συμβουλεύω ἐγὼ γνῶναι ὑμᾶς αὐτούς.
>
> "I advise you," he said, "men of the city, to know yourselves."[134]

It was also the lesson of the god of Delphi and of a man who, like Thrasyboulos, went down, at another time, to the Peiraieus.

But was it the lesson of Thucydides? It is clear that the *Hellenika* shows many of the same concerns as Thucydides' history of the Peloponnesian War. Both works display a continuing interest in the relation between thought, speech, and action; and both are equally absorbed in the conflict between passion and intelligence.[135] Xenophon shares Thucydides' conception of the importance of the role of the unexpected in human affairs and the inability of men finally to overcome it, especially in war. More particularly both works agree that Athens lost its empire and the war with Sparta more by its own doing than by Sparta's and that Sparta itself was never meant to be an imperial power.

And yet for all these similarities there obtains a fundamental difference of outlook which has nothing to do with Xenophon's failure to record the facts with Thucydidean precision.[136] Xenophon himself expresses the difference outright when he remarks, apropos of Theramenes' *bon mot*, that he has recorded something not worthy of mention *(ouk axiologa)*[137] and when he says at greater length, speaking of Teleutias' virtues as a commander:

> I am well aware, then, that in these incidents, I am recounting nothing worth mentioning about finance or danger or skillful plans. But, by god, it does seem worthwhile to me for a man to consider just what Teleutias did to affect thus his subordinates.[138]

Although Xenophon is by no means unconcerned in the *Hellenika* with money, danger, and tactics both military and diplomatic, it is also true that his concern with seemingly unimportant things is not limited to the relatively few places where he explicitly says he is. Nowhere does Thucydides show the interest Xenophon does, for example, in scenes like Thibron and his flute player, Mnasippos' high-handed dealing with his army, the embarassed entreaty made to Agesilaos by his son for Sphrodias, deaths like Anaxibios', or the encounter between Derkylidas and Meidias.[139] Perhaps it will not be too far-fetched to suggest that this prevailing interest in the less than impressive is signaled at the very opening of the work which ostensibly invites connection with Thucydides', for it contrasts markedly with the beginning of the undertaking it presumably carries forward. Thucydides' history begins with its author's name confidently stamping itself upon a record of events for which epical significance is claimed. If style is the man, the modesty and simplicity of Xenophon may betoken something more than the refinement of Greek rhetoric when placed beside the leonine and forbidding seriousness of his predecessor. Xenophon saw little of what he considered genuinely epic character in what he had to relate, not because the men and events he described were less imposing than those Thucydides was privileged to observe, but because he saw in their very quality and motivation, no matter their outcomes, something flawed at best and shabby at worst. Thus, too, the *Hellenika* is preeminently a history and not a type of mimetic literature—not a *Kyroupaideia*—because Xenophon in looking at the events of his time saw no norm worthy of imitation.

Though it will always be impossible to say for sure what Thucydides believed on a number of topics, because he died before he finished his work and because his ideas may have been in flux even as he wrote what he did, it seems safe to say that his admiration for the Athenian empire was genuine. The excesses of the People in governing their empire and themselves may have earned his censure, but he censured the idea of empire itself only so far as to agree with Perikles in opposing expansion during the War. He does not suggest that Athens lost an empire because of something inherent in imperialism but rather because of mistakes it made and unforeseen calamities it endured. In fact an attempt at Greek hegemony seems to him a necessary condition of the Athenian temper (and of any preeminent power) to the extent that Athens could not avoid being quite frankly the tyrant city.

In the *Hellenika* Xenophon expands the scope of his abiding concern with the relation of the individual and the city to examine the relation of city with city and the deeds of their leading men or those who wished to be and to confront that historial reality whose failure he appreciated but had conjured away at the beginning of the *Kyroupaideia*. And what he finds in the *Hellenika* is the same self-destructive force at work in the actions of cities and political and military men both illustrious and obscure as he had found in the actions of men seeking tyrannical power or as he saw finally implied in his imaginary Cyrus' pursuit of honors and fame. This, perhaps, may explain in part his interest in little men and seemingly insignificant deeds. Not only is he more anxious than Thucydides to make clear the varieties of emotion which can affect action, but he also wishes to throw into relief his questioning of Thucydides' intellectual and imperial assumptions. In the *Hellenika*, that is to say, Xenophon means to present a sobering account not of the decline of imperial grandeur but of imperialism's intrinsic and sometimes ignoble futility. Looking at the events of his time he could only conclude that when pursued with might and without regard for justice, the desire to have more inevitably led to having less. Even though energy and ambition could well be channeled in other directions, as Xenophon would show in the *Poroi*, it was the misfortune of his time to have found so alluring fifth-century Athens' example of power. Even if Epameinondas had lived or Sparta had remained in control, Xenophon would doubtless still have thought that aggressive seizure of power would sooner or later have its day of reckoning and provoke the assaults of others whom it had assaulted. No lasting polity in a city or productive peace among cities was conceivable when founded upon force or suppression gratuitously and constantly exerted. In the end Xenophon can confirm but amplify the notion of Thucydides, who saw as the true cause of the Peloponnesian War Spartan fear of Athenian growth and who saw in his analysis of *stasis* that the primary cause of political evil, especially in war, was the *pleonexia* and the *philotimia* of political and politicized individuals (Thuc. 3.82.8; cf. 1.75.3; 2.65.7).

The *Hellenika* is a relentless examination of the way things are, or rather the way most men think they are. Xenophon offers little hope for the improvement of a world inevitably involved with delusion; and the historian who scrupulously avoids using the term "common peace," the chief diplomatic instrument of the day, must be thought to have recognized the fundamental sham in a peace all too often concluded *faute de mieux*. If men's ambitions would inevitably increase with an increase in power, so much the worse. Xenophon probably expected few men to heed the advice Thrasyboulos gave, to understand that human desire must be regulated by a sense of limit and law. Indeed it may well be wondered if Thrasyboulos took his own advice; for he went forth to restore Athenian hegemony in the Hellespont only to die there as the chance victim of a mob enraged at the unruliness of his troops.[140] Even the carefully considered balance Kallistratos sought to achieve was too fragile to last for long, and it was helpless against an enemy when Epameinondas happened to be the foe.[141] Xenophon the historian, looking at the events of his time, presents in the *Hellenika* the uncertainty, ταραχή, of men and cities acting on unclear and erroneous beliefs, just as Socrates was recorded[142] to have entrapped men in a confusion which revealed their own misconceptions. Yet at the same time the *Hellenika* suggests a more difficult question for which there may not have been, and may still not be, an answer. Is justice possible in a frame of reference other than the *polis,* even at a period when, for better or worse, men actively seek a larger, more "cosmopolitan" scope of action?

So Lucian was right after all. Writing with more perspicacity than many since, he asserted that Xenophon was a "just historian," by which he meant impartial, as impartial as Thucydides.[143] But in calling Xenophon just, he said more than he ever realized.

7

XENOPHON AND ATHENS

> Rousseau said that Man is born free. Rousseau was wrong. No government of a civilized state can possibly regard its citizens as born free. On the contrary, it must regard them as born in debt, and as necessarily incurring fresh debt every day they live. . . . Not until it is paid can any freedom begin for the individual.
> — Shaw

Xenophon died sometime after 354, and Diogenes reports that the end came in Corinth, where Xenophon had fled when driven from Skillous by the resurgent Eleans in 371.[1] Many have accordingly believed that he never returned to Athens, even though his decree of exile had been rescinded, probably around 368.[2] But the fact that Xenophon may have died in Corinth does not mean that he actually lived there. In fact, as the *Hellenika* shows, it was rather unlikely, since it was Corinthians who engaged and set back an Athenian cavalry contingent (of which Xenophon's own sons were members) just prior to Mantineia,[3] and it was Corinthians who in 365 expelled an Athenian garrison from their city.[4] Would they have tolerated the presence of another Athenian who was now no longer in exile?

The Athens he returned to had changed considerably since the time he went off up-country with Cyrus. Militarily and diplomatically it had come back from the defeat of the Peloponnesian War, but its renewed attempts to regain its lost hegemony failed as other cities competed for supremacy in Greece or fiercely defended local interests. This quest by the cities for power and control over others provided a fitting backdrop for the search by individuals for a sense of personal identity and accomplishment which did not necessarily include a continuing respect for the political institutions of society. Autonomy was the slogan of the age, but new forms of tyranny were often its manifestation.

Professionalism was only one sign of the developing emphasis on individual achievement which made its own claims and could find an outlet for its own abilities anywhere, not just at home. The horizons of Greek life were expanding, and travel near and far in the name of professional diplomacy or for financial gain on mercenary service or in the pursuit of some other expertise became important. The sophistic movement had effected no small revolution. By insisting on the individual and his own responsibility for personal advance, it helped to break down further those ties of family and friend which were the basis of political life in most of the cities of Greece.[5] Yet even as they obtained an enormous liberation for individual enterprise, the sophists at the same time uprooted the individual from those ties of family and *polis* which once had given meaning to Hellenic life. If the family and the city were perceived as artificial groupings,[6] a chance assemblage of individual entities with no real and abiding connection, it is not surprising that the relations of men with one another increasingly became a matter of money and that the only genuine debts were monetary. The fee charged by the wandering teacher was emblematic.

Individual cities, no less than individual men, sought the same sort of self-advantage. The larger scope of Greek diplomacy in the fourth century was not, therefore, a groping towards a united Greek state but an ever-shifting jockeying for better chances at dominion or for protection against domination by others. Isokrates' talk of panhellenism was futile, babble in the wind. For all the assaults on its institutions, the *polis* remained an exclusive organization, which admitted outsiders with reluctance.[7] But it reaped the harvest of its own sowing when the disinclination of its citizens to work for it caused added financial burdens from the need to hire services, especially those of mercenaries to defend it.[8] As the *Hellenika* gives witness, lack of funds often bedevilled the very imperialism which was supposed to bring financial security, while peaceful isolationism often meant hardship for the many and invited inevitable aggression from abroad.

Perhaps it is in light of what Xenophon called the confusion of his time that the retrospective character of that age may best be understood. Early in the fourth century Praxagora in Aristophanes' *Ekklesiazousai* sings the praises of Athenian women by repeating as a refrain that they did everything "just like before,"[9] and the Chorus in the same play comments that gone are the days of Myronides, when no one dared to demand payment for guiding the city.[10] Isokrates' speeches, especially the *Panegyrikos*, are redolent of a nostalgic sentiment for the Greece of antiquity and the Persian wars, and Demosthenes later in the century conjured up more eloquently than any man a vision of their ancestral glory for his fellow Athenians.[11] Likewise in the visual arts, which saw the development of individual portraiture, an archaizing tendency simultaneously developed which bestowed upon shapes and designs a reminiscence of an older time when fourth-century Greeks doubtless imagined life was more simple and secure.[12] Yet it was just this sort of reverie which Perikles refused to indulge when he addressed his audience in 429, for the accomplishments of his own generation were more on his mind.[13] The fourth century, in spite of all its expertise, was not so confident. Travel away from the city or a concern within it for only private matters and an infatuation with the new and different seemed, if not to engender, at least to foster the opposite feelings for place and permanence. So in the *Ekklesiazousai* the Chorus comments on the audience's addiction to innovation,[14] while Xenophon reports in the *Memorabilia* how Hippias of Elis rebuked Socrates for always talking about the same things. Yet Socrates retorted that he not only talked about the same things but that he talked about them in the same way.[15]

Where did Xenophon stand in the tense atmosphere of these conflicting movements? There is no doubt that at one time, as a young man, he forsook the city of Athens in search of personal honor and glory abroad, even with Athens' enemies. But his own account of that journey shows both his disappointment in securing a permanent society away from the city and his understanding that success is only rarely the victory of the individual by himself. It is also worth noting his insistence in all of his Socratic works on Socrates' civic nature, especially on Socrates' concern that men of enterprising talent channel their energy towards the city's good and thus their own good as well. Xenophon, in other words, may have taken to heart the lesson he reports Socrates gave to Aristippos.[16] No man can continue to live happily by being a stranger everywhere. Indeed Xenophon's own use of the word *idiōtēs* to denote the private, as opposed to the public, person may have suggested to him the inadequacy of the radically private, since it also meant the undeveloped, the amateur, as opposed to the accomplished and fully mature master. Xenophon's return to Athens thus only befitted a student of Socrates, and it goes without saying that in an age which treasured up memories Xenophon should have treasured most the memory of Socrates. It was in Socrates where he found himself, and as he wrote in the *Memorabilia*, the recalling of that man when no longer present aided those who used to be with him and who welcomed his company.[17]

If Xenophon saw as an important part of Socrates' work the improving of men so that they were improved as citizens, it may be that he saw in his own work a similar aim. No record survives of Xenophon holding any office in Athens, but his own literary endeavors manifest a constant interest in the conduct of the *polis* and its members. The dating of these endeavors is a notoriously bootless task, but their times of composition can illuminate their connection with Athens. Eduard Schwartz made a most sensible observation when he remarked that the cross-references and repetitions in Xenophon's works imply that they were written more or less at the same time and under the same conditions.[18] Furthermore the works of Xenophon whose dates are relatively certain all were produced roughly between 368 and 354: The *Agesilaos* c. 360,[19] the *Poroi* c. 354,[20] the two treatises on equestrian matters in the mid-sixties,[21] the *Hiero* either in the sixties or even as late as 357,[22] and the

Kyroupaideia in the early sixties.[23] If the *Hellenika* can be accepted as unified in time of composition as well as in theme, it clearly had to be written after 362. Unfortunately there is no way to obtain an absolute date for the Socratic works, the *Constitution of the Lacedaemonians*, or the *Anabasis*; but nothing in them requires an early date, and there are some indications favoring a late one.[24] At any rate there is nothing unreasonable in thinking that these works fit the pattern of late dates set by the rest of the *oeuvre* and that Xenophon's literary effort belongs to the last decades of his life, the decades when he was in Athens. Xenophon the writer is therefore not the man who hunted and farmed abroad in Skillous, much less the man who fought for Cyrus, but the returned Socratic advising his fellow Athenians (and anyone else who cares to read) what he thinks best for the city.[25] Perhaps it was the influence of contact with other Socratics in Athens and the desire to put forth his own view of Socrates and the Socratic teaching which prompted his fast-paced literary output. But he did not have to be in Athens to have contact with philosophers, for Skillous was near Olympia, where he could often enjoy conversing with the wise. Perhaps, then, it was his reincorporation into the city which provided the necessary stimulation for his individual talent and inspired his evaluation of individualism and the political life. But return to the city did not mean unthinking allegiance. While it is clear that Xenophon had little use for the sophistic exaggeration of the private man's stature, he also refused to capitulate to blindly narrow patriotism. In the *Anabasis* he makes no overt apology for joining Cyrus, in the *Hellenika* he praises Athenian law and the restored democracy but hardly keeps hidden Athenian failures. In the *Agesilaos* he succeeds in doing what Socrates elsewhere called next to impossible: he praises a Spartan to Athenians (among others).[26] His thought, dedicated to meditation on the political and political virtue, is not the servant of "politics." Eschewing the radical independence of his earlier travel and the gratification of his own *philotimia*, he still retains a freedom from the narrow and partisan.

This independent attitude within an Athenian context is

also visible in the *Hipparkhikos,* the short essay on the duties of a cavalry commander, whose marked interest in the special state of the Athenian cavalry corps makes it highly unlikely that the work expresses home thoughts from abroad. It is a resolutely sober work whose blunt insistence is strange in Xenophon and may be owing to the genre of instructional literature to which the work belongs. It is as if Xenophon would encourage a sense of urgency and responsibility not only by discussing the duties of the horse officer but also by discussing them in a manner which is witness to their importance and which creates an atmosphere where there is no breathing space for lightheartedness.[27]

It is indicative of the tone of the whole piece that Xenophon everywhere emphasizes the duties of the cavalry commander and has next to nothing to say about his privileges. His responsibilities are in fact so great that the city, appreciating the difficulties, provides him with assistants to help him in his work.[28] His tasks run the gamut from practicing and improving his personal equestrian proficiency and that of his men, to obtaining what he needs from the authorities and, above all, defeating the enemy.[29] The demands incumbent on the hipparch are those typically required of Xenophon's leaders, but in the *Hipparkhikos* Xenophon stresses more the burdens of war and deception this public figure must carry. Even in the city he must use good speakers to placate the Council if it is angry,[30] and on festival days he seeks to obtain the Council's and the public's favor, as well as their entertainment, with maneuvres whose operation is calculated and kept skillfully concealed lest their exciting effect be lost on the observers.[31] This is a playful version of the deception the hipparch must work in earnest upon the enemy,[32] "for nothing is more profitable in war than deception,"[33] and most of the greatest advantages *(pleonektēmata)* in wars come from deceit.[34] In fact Xenophon suggests that there is a necessary connection between the public commander, war, and trickery:

> Therefore either a man ought not to attempt to lead or he must ask the gods for this ability [to deceive] in addition to his other qualities and must contrive to possess it himself.[35]

Xenophon does not imply, however, that the cavalry commander is an aggressor; he is a war expert, not a warmonger. When Xenophon says, therefore, that no art should be as assiduously practiced as the military art,[36] he is recognizing that the city must of necessity be involved in the use of force and sometimes aim to harm if it is to obtain or preserve its own happiness. But this is not to say that he approves of militarism, for, as he shows in the *Hellenika*, war, especially imperialist war, is risky and can obviously lead to ruin. The sensible commander does not take unnecessary risks, except when he will clearly have an advantage *(pleon hexei)* beforehand over the enemy.[37] He will not provoke enemies, let alone encourage their multiplication.

Xenophon finds that the glory of command resides in its toil, and the hipparch's goal as a public official is the reduction of the enemy to the status of an *idiōtēs*, a private layman.[38] Xenophon does not minimize the rigors of the position, he makes no attempt to glamorize it falsely. And he is not reluctant to state openly several times that few men will heed what he says or do what is proper.[39] Xenophon has no illusions about the nature of his audience. Though concerned with the city's good, he feels no need to flatter its citizens. He refuses to convince by coddling. His relation to the city becomes more clear. Like his Socrates, who once gave advice to an aspirant to the post of hipparch,[40] Xenophon gives similar instruction; but just as Socrates was hardly a knight, Xenophon was not a hipparch. Both men were concerned for the city's good, but neither saw his task as the personal performance of public exploits. Socrates by his loving spirit and devotion to the truth was disqualified from the warrior's office;[41] Xenophon by his hard candor in the *Hipparkhikos* differentiates himself from the commander who has to be an adept in deception. Xenophon's activity as a citizen is precisely to think, to write, to recommend. It is to the city and his fellow Athenians that he here directs his energy; and so it may be that for all his military interests and accomplishments, like Socrates he came to a perception of his life and himself which led not to the pacifist but to the pacific.

Xenophon, of course, was an equestrian, and it was an encounter with a horse which taught his Socrates about his own value and virtue.[42] In the horse Xenophon and Socrates are met. Unlike the Pheidippides of the *Clouds*, they both can be said to have possessed what the lingo of the American West calls horse sense. Xenophon's contemplation of equine matters in the *Peri Hippikēs* is at once a companion piece to the *Hipparkhikos* and a remarkable example of a technical treatise infused with a philosophic spirit. It serves to locate further Xenophon's position in the world of ideas of fourth-century Athens and Greece.

Xenophon is aware that horsemanship might be considered an idle pastime, and he knows that horsebreaking especially is indulged in by those better employed in the affairs of home and city.[43] He presents in the *Art of Horsemanship* what is the genuine virtue of equestrian mastery and does it in such a way that he underlines the ties binding the excellent man and the training of the excellent horse.[44] Both are free and work willingly, both are pleasing and awesome things to behold. The horse only becomes such by being directed in a rigorous and orderly fashion, even as a man requires constant practice and conditioning. The successful training process for both also depends not so much on compulsion as on persuasion. A horse knows no more to do what is right when compelled than a dancer learns rhythm by being beaten or whipped in time.[45] Furthermore the anger of a horse when provoked is as ruinous as a man's; and a horse, Xenophon says, ought never to be approached by a man who is himself in an angry temper.[46] There is a kinship, in other words, between rider and mount (it is interesting to note how Xenophon uses analogies from things human to clarify points of instruction)[47] which should be guided by a spirit of affability between them. An unruly animal harms both itself and its master, and both must exercise together if both are to be mutually useful and save each other from trouble.[48] The equestrian who neglects his horse neglects himself, for in time of danger he entrusts his bodily well-being to it.[49]

This emphasis on the friendliness which supports the relation of man and beast sets off the *Peri Hippikēs* from the more brusk *Hipparkhikos*. That essay, concerned with enemies and the difficulties of command, has a martial spirit which contrasts sharply with the amiability of its companion piece. The *Peri Hippikēs* stresses that peaceful spirit of personal endeavor and personal achievement the private person enjoys; and it is the private person, the *idiōtēs*, whom Xenophon here addresses.[50] Even as a work of literature the treatise possesses its own amiability, for Xenophon intends it especially for his young friends.[51] Moreover he graciously salutes his predecessor in the subject, Simon, at the same time as his own Greek certainly surpasses in charm and verve the crabbed clumsiness of the fifth-century expert.[52]

The *Peri Hippikēs*, like Xenophon's Socrates, delights as it instructs. But it does more insofar as it suggests that the equestrian student, in learning to train and develop a horse, learns to benefit himself. The horse, even as it is trained, becomes itself the vehicle of instruction. As Socrates maintained, there is no better way to become excellent than by following the way which leads to excellence.[53] The systematic patience needed to develop the horse can only aid the further development of the master. It is interesting on this account to observe how Xenophon structures the essay so that he follows both the anatomy of the animal and its growth in time from the hour of purchase to the day of full maturity. For in the progress of time and growth there is more than chronological or quantitative development; at the end of Xenophon's discussion the horse has been transformed into the steed of the gods and heroes, and the man who rides using his steed well becomes himself outstanding. His excellence brings him glorious repute.[54]

But he also has the potential to be useful to the city. His ability with horses teaches him the rudiments of proper economy, for he will want to make his horses better than when he first receives them.[55] Finally the good rider knows how to defend himself from attack;[56] he will be able, if led properly, to defend the city. Indeed if he is a cavalry commander, he will be more concerned with his troop's splendor than his own.[57] Xenophon's thought has come full circle, as he is aware when he concludes the *Peri Hippikēs* with an explicit reference to the *Hipparkhikos*.[58] It is not that every individual is to become a leading public figure, but that the growth of the individual seems to include a public dimension. As Xenophon says, he does not recommend horsebreaking because it will turn the horsemen's attention from what is important, namely, public interests.[59]

In writing a technical treatise Xenophon was hardly being innovative. Not to mention Simon, Xenophon's own fourth-century contemporary Ainaios Taktikos was only one of many who were writing on military manoeuvres and a variety of topics in a spirit congruent with the increase of professionalism. But just as Xenophon in the *Agesilaos* made of the biographical encomium a form peculiarly his own, so in the *Peri Hippikēs* he adds an unmistakably personal element. In the *Memorabilia* he records how Socrates criticized as too narrow the view of a teacher of generalship that tactics was the be-all and the end-all of command.[60] In his own treatise on horses Xenophon manifests a similarly broad concern for a particular activity; perhaps directly attempting to overcome the illiberal strictures of the specialist, he seeks to discover in the technical something satisfying and beneficial to the expert as a man, not merely as a professional. His fascination with the details of equestrian training and regimen stems not only from a desire for textbook accuracy but also from a fascination with order in general and the perception that progress through an ordered and beneficent program leads to individual improvement in more than the one thing mastered. Xenophon as a Socratic incorporates the specialized outlook into a larger vision and repudiates by implication the teaching of skill without substance, virtuosity without understanding. In so doing, he doubtless sought to aid by his advice all who were interested, just as his teacher before him had done. And even though the *Peri Hippikēs* speaks to the private person, it does not present an invitation to the gratuitous exploitation of equestrian skills. Like Socrates, Xenophon does not encourage the mad passion of a Pheidippides but the careful nurturing of an ability useful to the city as well as the self.

Xenophon addressed Athens directly in one other work, the last he wrote, the *Poroi*; in it he formulates for the city a policy of ways and means after the devastating and costly defeat of the Social War. Like the good commander he so often thinks about, who provides for his troops, Xenophon proposes methods of providing for his fellow citizens in this tract of peace. With all its concrete plans it reveals Xenophon in an individual capacity working for the city's good, and thus it sums up, as it puts into practice, all that he has written. It is typical of its author that it looks to the nature of Attika itself for a solution to Attika's problems and to the promise for improvement the city's own soil, climate, and geographical position possess.[61] Xenophon stresses as well the necessity for the Athenians themselves to work at making the city as attractive as possible to industrious resident aliens and foreign commercial interests.[62] But it is not imports which will give the city its greatest source of revenue; it is, rather, the profit which will derive from the increased exploitation of its own silver mines.[63] Athens' power, directed to self-awareness, will flow from within, and city and citizens will aid each other in bearing costs and sharing profits. Once again Xenophon sees no conflict between private and public interest when he answers the objections of those who fear too much state involvement:

> ... rather, just as allies, to the extent they come together more, make each other more strong, so in the silver mines to the extent that more work, to that extent will they find and take out more good things.[64]

The *Poroi* is not, therefore, like Isokrates' *On The Peace*, a call to Athens to retreat from its international position or to give up its enterprising spirit.[65] Xenophon does not seek the impossible but only the redirection of the city's energy away from wars of foreign conquest and towards an economic hegemony which can only last as long as peace lasts. As he frequently emphasizes, history has shown that prosperity is jeopardized by the coercion of others, since force induces risky and costly conflict. Clearly with the conclusion of the *Hellenika* in mind, he claims:

> But right now, owing to the confusion in Greece (*tēn en tēi*

helladi tarakhēn), it seems to me the chance has befallen the city to regain the Greeks for itself without toils and without dangers and without cost.⁶⁶

None of this is to deny that military strength must be maintained. Yet Xenophon shrewdly argues that its use would of necessity diminish, because Athens would have in its debt so many foreigners that an aggressor would fail for want of allies. In the rigorous avoidance of doing wrong to others *(adikountes)*, Athens would probably be less wronged itself.⁶⁷ Its self-reliance would bring it commanding security.

If the *Poroi* reveals a typically Xenophontic habit of mind in its actual proposals, it also reveals his custom of grounding his views upon more than the immediate problem or situation. For the *Poroi* is not fundamentally a political pamphlet propagandizing for one policy over another so much as it is a reflection on the relation between economics, the city, and justice.⁶⁸ The *Poroi* does not confront Athens' fiscal situation to the exclusion of the other elements of its life. Xenophon remarks at the very outset that leaders, though they claim to know what is just, often engage in injustice at the expense of other cities, because they must obtain for their people vital necessities, not all of which may be available at home.⁶⁹ He attempts to discover how Athens can provide for its own people with its own resources, material and mental, so as to dispel the suspicion with which others regard it. Self-knowledge is once again revealed as the basic constituent of proper growth; the teaching of Socrates is reaffirmed by an essay which realizes that economics is a part of politics, the life of the city.

Wealthy Kallias in the *Symposium* declares that money makes men just.⁷⁰ Xenophon in the *Poroi* does not make the same claim; he is not an economic moralist. What he does say is that through self-economy Athens will be less unjust before the world and will be engaged in a just activity. But Xenophon is aware that men often do things for other than economic motives, that honor and glory may often require more loss than gain. Money may render men more capable of justice, but it cannot make them just.⁷¹ To forget this is to forget the lesson of the financially insignificant Socrates, the most just of men, and the example of the younger Cyrus, whose princely birth did not prevent his becoming a rebel. It would clearly be ridiculous, however, for the city to insist on the virtue of poverty; too few are called to appreciate its pleasures. Instead the *Poroi* advises the satisfaction of want in such a way that men will not seek to reach out for more because they will no longer feel as much the need for more, being content, it is to be hoped, with enough. Xenophon's economics is thus essentially antiimperialist. It bears out the lesson of the *Hellenika*, just as it carries the stamp of a Socratic mind hostile to excess and seeking concord where it may.[72]

But Xenophon was now nobody's fool. If he had nothing else, he had the example of Socrates to convince him that the city did not always do the right thing at the right time. This of course did not deter him, just as it had not deterred Socrates, from doing and saying what he thought was proper. Above all he had little sympathy with those who foolishly engaged in risk or who left everything to luck or the gods, in despair of human power to achieve success or in disregard of human power for calculation. Thus the foolish love of Kritoboulos in the *Symposium* and the *Memorabilia* is juxtaposed with an acrobatic leaping over up-turned sword points, breathtaking, no doubt, but ultimately dangerous, a flirtation with death, not the true love of the thinking life.[73] That Xenophon writes a technical treatise or investigates finance attests to his continuing affirmation of skill over chance and sense over infatuation, and he would have shared his contemporary Timotheos' resentment when that general's success was attributed to fortune.[74] By the same token Socrates in the *Memorabilia* counsels that a man should do all he can with his own powers before seeking the aid of the divine.[75] It is this self-reliance which makes Xenophon emerge as a dashing figure for all his reticence and which endows many of his works with a sharp vitality. He was clearly a man who enjoyed graceful accomplishment, physical as well as mental, and whose admiration for robustness and style must have alienated him from a place like the Academy with its prissily uniformed students and exalted but stooped-over master.⁷⁶ Xenophon always feared and suspected the possibility of pretense in grandeur; as his own style bears witness, he liked his designs lean and simple.

He was also a man with an independent mind which refused to reject the value of old beliefs when confronted with new ideas and developments. He admired, to be sure, innovators like Iphikrates or Epameinondas and was himself instrumental in developing prose as a lucid vehicle of expression; and he was prompt at mastering new literary forms and making innovations of his own. His language, for all its Attic honey so impartial in its use of words from other dialects, looks forward to the Greek which would flourish in the new age inaugurated by Alexander. Yet Xenophon was not a revolutionary, and his attitude, like that of many men who straddle two eras, seems to have tried to reconcile the fresh and recent, the "modern," with a heritage as old as Greece itself, a reconciliation he saw embodied in the teaching of Socrates. When he finally came to write, it seems mature reflection would not allow him to accept the claims of the thoroughgoing individualism so prevalent in his time; his intellectual effort was directed towards finding a way of integrating the excellence of the singular within the structure of the many, just as his style sought to achieve a harmonious unity out of a continuing respect for the value of the individual detail and the individual word. Xenophon does not propose any radical changes in Greek or Athenian life the way another Socratic pupil would, but he does not call for a simple-minded return to a romantically improved past either. Rather he aims at enlightening the present with a sense of the timeless. He seeks out the typical, not the antiquated; and though he can bestir men with glowing rhetoric about the accomplishments of their forefathers,⁷⁷ he looks to the past more for corroboration than inspiration.⁷⁸

And yet, for all his confident intellectual awareness, there is in Xenophon a profound feeling of human inadequacy and a sense, never forgotten, that permanence and perfection always elude. Even as he describes the ultimate success of the horseman, he comments that a spirit may thwart further glory,[79] just as Socrates tells the promising Kallias at the end of the *Symposium* that the god might harm.[80] In the *Hipparkhikos* Xenophon repeatedly urges the need for devotion to the gods and can answer critics of his opinion by saying that only the gods know all, while men, especially men in perilous undertakings, rarely can foresee the outcome of their plans.[81] It is for this reason as well that he writes only notes, *hypomnēmata*, since it is impossible to spell out everything a commander will have to face,[82] just as in the *Memorabilia* he will stress the need for householders and governors to consult the gods, since they are inevitably involved, by the nature of their occupations, in taking risks and in performing deeds which are uncertain in their result.[83] A rationalistic mind will always find this perception of reality hard to appreciate, but Xenophon should not be thought to mean that the gods manipulate man, let alone that man, by some magic, can manipulate the gods. The gods are the final expression of Xenophon's belief that the individual is not self-sufficient; to him their worship is the best reminder of human limitation. Typically, his attitude is as old as Homer and Hesiod, if not as old as man. The attainment of excellence requires something more than human agency, an agency whose epiphanies will always be transient. For Xenophon a man can overcome his limitation only by a respect for those very deities which confirm his continuing imperfection.

The same can be said for the city. Success for city and citizens depends upon the honest evaluation of self, which can best be seen in the light of the infinitely great and all-powerful. Perhaps it is for this reason that Xenophon at the end of the *Poroi* requests his fellow Athenians not to take his suggestions on his word alone. He counsels them, as Socrates once counselled him, to ask the Oracle whether his plan is good or bad and then, and only then, which gods will best insure its happy outcome.[84] As a young man he deliberately did not make the first inquiry in his eagerness to be off up-country. The old man is wiser. The god is not mocked, and it is pleasing, even if not deliberately intended, that the *Poroi*, which begins *egō* (I) ends with *polei* (for the city).

It is possibly the last word Xenophon wrote and probably the last he published. A coincidence, no doubt, but a fitting fate.

The exile had returned, sage now, as well as heroic.

ABBREVIATIONS

Ages.	Agesilaos
Anab.	Anabasis
Apol.	Apology
CofL	Constitution of the Lacedaemonians
Kyro.	Kyroupaideia
Hell.	Hellenika
Hi.	Hiero
Hipp.	Hipparkhikos
Mem.	Memorabilia
Oik.	Oikonomikos
P.H.	Peri Hippikēs
Por.	Poroi

NOTES

Chapter 1

1. *Mem.* 1.3.13.
2. Barthold Georg Niebuhr, "Über Xenophons Hellenika," *Rheinisches Museum* 1 (1827), pp. 194ff. Also in *Kleine historische und philosophische Schriften* (Bonn, 1828), Vol. 1, pp. 464ff.
3. Cf. Leo Strauss, *On Tyranny* (London, 1963), p. 110, note 3.
4. *Decline and Fall,* chapter 24, at note 24 in the Bury edition.
5. Olaf Gigon, *Kommentar zum ersten Buch von Xenophons Memorabilien* (Basel, 1953), p. 2.
6. *Mem.* 4.6.13.
7. *Anab.* 4.3.11. This and all other translations from the Greek, as well as from scholarly prose in modern languages, are original.
8. *Anab.* 4.5.32.
9. *Sym.* 4.27.
10. *Sym.* 4.25.
11. *Ages.* 1.23.
12. On this point in general and for the following examples in particular, cf. Léopold Gautier, *La langue de Xénophon* (Geneva, 1911), p. 151.
13. Cf. Plutarch, *Artaxerxes* 8.1, apropos of Xenophon's description of Kounaxa.
14. *Kyro.* 7.1.37. Cf. Longinus, *On the Sublime* 25.4. A striking partial similarity with this scene can be found in the visual arts in the famous Dexileos stele commemorating a young man fallen at Koroneia.
15. *Hell.* 4.5.7.
16. *Anab.* 4.7.24-5.
17. *Kyro.* 6.4.3.
18. Hippolyte Taine, "Xénophon: L'Anabase," in *Essais de critique et d'histoire,* second edition (Paris, 1866), pp. 149 and 129. It is also interesting how Taine sees in Xenophon a habit of perception and expression unlike the modern world's. (Cf. Strauss' remark, *On Tyranny,* p. 198, that admirers of Jane Austen have an easier access to Xenophon than those who prefer Dostoevsky). For what it is worth, it should also be remembered that Taine was eager to rehabilitate the reputation of Mozart's

operas. Perhaps it is not too wild to suggest that an age which could not appreciate the lucidity, grace, and profound humor of Mozart was at least consistent in its disregard for the similar qualities of Xenophon.

19. Cf., e.g., *Anab.* 4.3.7 where the anaphora conveys the sense of mounting despair as the Greeks count up the obstacles in their way, or *Hell.* 4.3.19 where the asyndeton and isocola, alliteration and homoioteleuton, far from gratuitously adorning the description of Koroneia, depict the tough and evenly balanced progress of the battle, distilling the action to an almost balletic purity of motion.

20. Cf. the penetrating remark of Paul Friedländer, *Plato*, English trans., (New York, 1958), vol. 1, p. 136: "The question — seen as a demand for clarity and a turning of the Socratic existence toward the object itself (and turning, at the same time, the disciple toward the same object) — already contained the answer in a very definite sense."

21. Thus he has been compared in the visual arts not to Hellenistic models but to the controlled emotion and individualization of Parrhasios and of the Lyme Park relief. Cf. T.B.L. Webster, *Art and Literature in Fourth Century Athens* (London, 1956), pp. 17-8.

22. Homer achieves a comparable effect in the famous scene in *Iliad* 6. 495 by simply describing Andromakhe's continuing backward glances towards Hektor.

23. For the opposite view that Xenophon could not, because of his fascination with the particular, see how things hung together as a whole, cf. Wilhelm Prinz, *De Xenophontis Cyri Institutione* (Göttingen, 1911), pp. 55-6.

24. Just this failure of insight can be seen, for example, in H.D. Westlake, "Individuals in Xenophon, *Hellenica*," *Bulletin of the John Rylands Library* 49 (1966): 246ff. (now in *Essays on the Greek Historians and Greek History* [Manchester, 1969], pp. 203ff.) and in Hans Breitenbach, "Die Seeschlacht bei Notion," *Historia* 20 (1971): 152ff. It is worthwhile to recall the remark of Mathias Hemardinquer, *La Cyropédie* (Paris, 1872), p. 40. which, if it goes a bit too far, errs in the right direction: "It seems that Xenophon composed his writings on the model of the conversations of Socrates, free, rapid, touching on all subjects, with an interior unity but without visible connection, always unforeseen, lovely as much as just, removed from all that which could resemble a methodical composition, book or discourse."

25. *Hell.* 6.3.4.
26. 6.3.3.
27. 6.2.32.
28. 3.5.5.
29. *Anab.* 2.5.3ff.
30. 2.5.7.
31. Paul Masqueray, Budé *Anab.* (Paris, 1930), *ad loc.*
32. There is even a dissertation on the subject by Fortunatus Schnyder, *Die Religiosität Xenophons* (Basel, 1953).

33. E.g., Anab. 2.1.9.
34. Anab. 2.1.15ff., 2.4.19.
35. Hell. 1.6.1ff.
36. 1.6.4.
37. 1.5.6.
38. 1.6.7.
39. Cf., e.g., Hans Breitenbach, Historiographische Anschauungsformen Xenophons (Basel, 1950), p. 108.
40. Hell. 1.6.4.
41. 1.6.15.
42. Ibid.
43. 1.6.33.
44. 2.3.56.
45. Apol. 28.
46. Oik. 8.20.
47. Cf. the survey by Otto Ribbeck, "Über den Begriff des εἴρων," Rheinisches Museum 31 (1876): 381ff., esp. p. 387.
48. Nikomakhean Ethics 4.7, 1127b30. Also, cf. Kyro. 2.2.12.
49. NE, 2.7, 1108a20; 4.7, 1127b8.
50. Ibid., 4.7, 1127b23.
51. Friedländer, Plato, p. 153.
52. Cf., e.g., the praise at Mem. 4.8.11.
53. Mem. 4.1.1.
54. Aristotle, NE 4.3, 1124b30.
55. Cf., e.g., the fundamental study by Ivo Bruns, Das literarische Porträt der Griechen (Berlin, 1896), pp. 383-413, and the introduction to the Budé Sym. (Paris, 1961) by François Ollier, pp. 9ff.
56. Sym. 1.1.
57. Ollier, introduction to the Budé Sym., by contrast believes the theme of the Sym. is not love but the noble and the good, (kalokagathia). For a reply, which recognizes the centrality of love in the work but does not see its significance in the way it is seen here, cf. Robert Flacelière, "A propos du Banquet de Xénophon," Revue des Études Grecques 54 (1961): 93ff.
58. Mem. 4.1.2.
59. Sym. 4.18-20.
60. 5.1ff. For the light, cf. 5.2. and 5.9.
61. 1.3-5.
62. 6.6-8.
63. 2.14-7.
64. 6.1ff.
65. 8.12. Cf. Leo Strauss, Xenophon's Socrates (Ithaca, 1972), p. 172.
66. Sym. 4.34ff., esp. 4.44.
67. 8.6.
68. Cf. the rebuke of Socrates to Antisthenes at Diogenes Laertios 2.36.
69. Sym. 3.4, 3.6, 4.3.

70. 3.6, 4.5; cf. also 2.7. If Joel had read the *Symposium* with more attention (as well as *Mem.* 2.5) he might never have conceived his theory that Xenophon's understanding of Socrates derives from Antisthenes. He would have spared himself the effort of writing his monumental *Der echte und der xenophontische Sokrates* (Berlin, 1893) and spared others the effort of having to read it.

71. *Sym.* 4.21. Cf. the wise notion of the Spartans, approved by Socrates, that lovers of Kritoboulos' sort may be a danger to an army because they might be good only as long as their beloveds survive or stay with them (8.35).

72. 8.3.

73. 2.3.

74. 4.55.

75. For which he is rebuked by Socrates, 6.8-10.

76. 1.13ff.

77. 4.29ff.

78. 4.31-2.

79. *Hell.* 2.3.2, 2.3.39.

80. *Sym.* 7.2-5. This signals the coming discourse on love and the switch from comments about beauty and love made by people like Kritoboulos. On the connection between this sort of attraction and the Syracusan's presentation of juggling, somersaulting over knives, etc., cf. the discussion in the presence of Kritoboulos at *Mem.* 1.3.9-10.

81. 3.10.

82. 8.1.

83. 8.2.

84. 8.30.

85. 8.33ff.

86. 8.10, 8.25. The way Socrates' sense of humor differs from Philip's is akin to that between two sorts of comedy, between, for example, the *Clouds* and the *Symposium*. Cf. Aristotle, *NE* 4.8, 1128a20, who says that to the authors of old comedy indecency of language was amusing, whereas to the authors of the newer sort of comedy, i.e., Xenophon's contemporaries, innuendo was more pleasing. The two differ in no small way in their regard for propriety.

87. *Sym.* 8.9-10.

88. 8.6, 8.12ff.

89. 8.20ff.

90. 8.18, 8.25-7.

91. 8.42.

92. 8.41.

93. So he can call them all lovers at the beginning of his discourse, 8.1.

94. 9.1.

95. There is no good reason, especially considering the nature of the rest of the company, to doubt this identification, as Ollier, introduction to the Budé *Sym.*, p. 28, does.

96. *Sym.*, 2.26-7.

97. It is to be noted that only Socrates engages in a dialogue to establish his point about his occupation. On the connection between dialogic speech and genuine love, cf. 8.18.

98. 4.56ff, esp. 4.59-60. Everyone signals his agreement to Socrates' queries by saying *panu men oun* (why,yes), but Socrates eventually asks the question whether a man who makes his clients suitable to one person or to many is preferable. Some at the party give the right answer, the man who pleases many, while the rest answer nonsensically "why yes." It should also be noted that, befitting a friendly party, Socrates uses a dialogic method which proceeds by agreement, not by cross examination. For a (typically) different reading of this passage, cf. Strauss, *Xenophon's Socrates*, p. 164.

99. 9.6-7.

100. The importance of these personalities for an interpretation of the *Symposium* has been recognized by Strauss, *Xenophon's Socrates*, p. 169.

101. *Sym.* 8.43.

102. So Nikeratos, for example, for all his knowledge of Homer, seems not to realize that Socrates does not quote Homer exactly, at least as Homer's text is now preserved. Like so much else in his discourse, Socrates makes the best of the poet and elicits what Xenophon and other Socratics would call the ὑπόνοια or "undermeaning" of Homer's poetry.

103. 9.7.

104. 1.1. Xenophon's presence is only "literary." He was in fact about five years old in 422, the temporal setting of Kallias' banquet.

Chapter 2

1. Diogenes Laertios 2.48.

2. Jean Luccioni, *Les idées politiques et sociales de Xénophon* (Paris, 1947), p. 21.

3. Cf. Werner Jaeger, *Paideia*, English trans., (New York, 1944), Vol. 3, p. 156.

4. Diogenes Laertios 2.50, based upon *Anab.* 3.1.4-7.

5. *Antigonos von Karystos* in *Philologische Untersuchungen* 4 (1884) appendix 4.

6. 2.51 and 2.58.

7. *Hell.* 3.1.4.

8. 6.1ff. (Bartoletti).

9. *Hell.* 3.1.6; *Anab.* 7.8.24.

10. 5.6.3.

11. 8.1.

12. *History of Greece*, 1856 ed., Vol. 9, p. 242, note 1.

13. Edouard Delebecque, *Essai sur la vie de Xénophon* (Paris, 1957), p. 123.

14. *Anab.* 3.1.5. The argument of Hans Breitenbach, "Xenophon," article in Pauly-Wissowa-Kroll, *Realencyclopädie der Altertumswissenschaft,* Vol. 18, second series, col. 1774, that this passage has nothing to do, even by implication, with Xenophon's exile but is an attempt to exonerate Socrates from connection with his disciple's treason fails to be convincing. The whole point of the episode is to show that Socrates was right about something Xenophon erred in, and that "something" was the expedition of Cyrus. On the basis of this passage alone, of course, no date can be established for the exile; but the passage becomes otiose in the Anabasis, if it has, as Breitenbach seems to imply, nothing to do with what the *Anab.* is all about.

15. *Anab.* 5.3.7ff., where the form of the verb *pheugein,* whether aorist or imperfect indicative, may better be translated "escaped the danger" rather than the usual "was in exile." Cf. Hartmut Erbse, "Xenophons Anabasis," *Gymnasium* 73 (1966): 491-2; also Delebecque, *Essai sur la vie de Xénophon,* p. 120.

16. *Anab.* 7.7.57.

17. Delebecque, *Essai sur la vie de Xénophon,* p. 121; Hans Baden, *Untersuchungen zur Einheit der Hellenika Xenophons* (Hamburg, 1966), p. 46. Eduard Schwartz, "Quellenuntersuchungen zur griechischen Geschichte," *Rheinisches Museum* 44 (1899): 168 (also in *Gesammelte Schriften* [Berlin 1956], p. 144) obelizes the passage, since he considered it fatal for the 394 date he favored. Yet it must be admitted that, no matter how fitting an earlier reference seems here, *ou gar pō,* considered generally, does not necessarily have to refer to something imminent. Cf., e.g., the opening of the *Prometheus* where the deliverer is said not yet to have been born (1.27), a deliverer who will only come in thirteen generations.

18. Schwartz, "Quellenuntersuchungen", pp. 164ff. (pp. 140-141 in *Gesammelte Schriften*), comments on the comparatively numerous details in the *Hell.* about cavalry activity during the tyranny at Athens and concludes that Xenophon must have been an eyewitness and participant as a knight. Xenophon's ability as a horseman is indisputable, and it is known that the knights as a class fought with the oligarchs during the stasis in Athens at the close of the fifth century. Cf. *Hell.* 2.4.2ff.

19. Erbse, "Xenophons Anabasis," p. 495.

20. He may also have had, like Socrates, a troublesome wife, if a dialogue of Aischines of Sphettos, the *Aspasia,* is to be believed.

21. For Plato, cf. esp. the famous passage in the Seventh Epistle 324b-326b.

22. On Polykrates it is convenient—and safe—to consult Anton-Hermann Chroust, *Socrates: Man and Myth* (London, 1957), pp. 69ff. More recently, cf. the important article by H. Erbse, "Die Architectonik im Aufbau von Xenophons Memorabilien," *Hermes* 89 (1961): 261ff.

23. Demonstrated by Erbse, "Die Architectonik," pp. 257ff., p. 286. Note also the *Mem.'s* last word, *krinetō,* "let him judge." Erbse also goes a long way to reestablishing the unity of the *Mem.* against those who

would separate off from the rest the so-called *Schutzschrift*, Bk. 1.1-1.2. That the *Mem.* is not just a hodgepodge of random little dialogues may also be learned from a reading of Leo Strauss' running narrative commentary in *Xenophon's Socrates* (Ithaca, 1972).

24. This is not to justify, however, the assumption made in the past that Xenophon intended his Socratic works for actual publication as one ensemble.

25. *Mem.* 2.1.1ff.

26. This is an important shift in the direction of the argument, though evolving organically from what preceded. The MSS division of books can therefore be accepted, against the view of those who would include the dialogue with Aristippos with what is now Book One (cf., e.g., Breitenbach, "Xenophon," col. 1795, and Strauss, *Xenophon's Socrates*, pp. 32ff.). That book seems concerned more generally with Socrates' own character and not, like Books Two and Three, with how Socrates specifically aided his friends and interlocutors. Book One in fact recalls in its organization Xenophon's biographical encomium of Agesilaos, since both begin, when discussing virtues, with comments on each man's piety, and both end with comments on how each man was not a braggart. On the Socratics and biography, cf. Arnaldo Dante Momigliano, *The Development of Greek Biography* (Cambridge, Mass., 1971), pp. 46ff.

27. 2.1.11-3.

28. 2.1.15.

29. *Politics* 1.2, 1253a.

30. *Mem.* 2.1.21ff. Strauss, *Xenophon's Socrates*, pp. 37-8, sees, however, a third option silently implicit—the life of Socrates which, he maintains, is a viable *via media* unlike Aristippos'.

31. 2.1.30-2.

32. 2.1.4. Cf. also the remarks of Olaf Gigon, *Kommentar zum zweiten Buch von Xenophons Memorabilien* (Basel, 1956), p. 33.

33. 2.2.13. Cf. Aristotle, *Nikomakhean Ethics* 5.5, 1133a1-5, on the importance of gratitude as one of the essential graces of civic life. Xenophon would naturally have had little sympathy for the theory (which would have struck him as a form of sophism) that the individual was his own owner and owed nobody anything. On this theory, cf. C.B. Macpherson, *The Political Theory of Possessive Individualism* (Oxford, 1962).

34. 2.2.14.

35. 2.3.18-9.

36. 2.4.7.

37. 2.6.21-2.

38. 2.6.23-6.

39. 2.6.24-5.

40. 2.6.21 and 23.

41. It should be noticed that Xenophon's structural progression in Book Two of the *Mem.* is similar to the progression Aristotle sees in nature: Cf. *Politics*, 1.2, 1252b-1253a, where the development is teleological at least in

history. For an interesting, if not wholly convincing, discussion of the problem of the meaning of familial and social vis-a-vis the political, cf. Hannah Arendt, *The Human Condition* (Chicago, 1958), pp. 22-37.

42. *Oik.* 8.3.
43. 8.12-7.
44. 6.8-10, although this does not mean such men are to be busybodies or political hacks. Iskhomakhos does not normally "hang out" in town.
45. 7.30.
46. 16.3.
47. 14.1ff., 7.15.
48. 14.8-9.
49. *Mem.* 3.4.12. Contrast Aristotle, *Pol.* 1.1, 1252a and the comment of Aquinas, *Summa Theo.* 2.2.58.7, ad 2.
50. *Mem.* 4.4.18.
51. 3.12.1ff.
52. 3.7.9. This dialogue may shed some light on the nature of Xenophon's activity in the *Mem.* Since Kharmides was one of the Thirty Tyrants, Xenophon's including a conversation with such an associate of Socrates in his defense of Socrates shows he was not reluctant to include things democrats in Athens may have considered grist for their mill. But at the same time the conversation is hardly "featured," being carefully placed deep within the central part of the entire work.
53. 1.4.5ff.
54. 1.4.12.
55. 4.3.11-2.
56. 4.4.24-5.
57. Contrast *Mem.* 1.1.1 and Plato, *Apology* 24b8-24c1. Cf. *Mem.* 1.3.1-4 and 1.3.5ff, 1.4 and 1.5, 4.3, 4.4 and 4.5. Leo Strauss, *Xenophon's Socrates*, p. 18 and *passim* also perceives this structural principle at work. For the priority of the gods, cf. also *Oik.* 11.8, *Ages.* 3.1, *Hipp.* 1.1, *Kyro.* 1.5.14.
58. *Mem.* 1.4.11 and 15. On possible implications of this, cf. Strauss, *Xenophon's Socrates*, pp. 24-6.
59. *Oik.* 5.7.
60. 6.1. Cf. the agricultural prayer of the elder Cato to Mars, *de agri cultura* 141.
61. 4.4ff.
62. 5.13-4.
63. *Mem.* 2.6.21-2.
64. *Oik.* 17.4.
65. 8.16.
66. 5.18. Marchant, followed by Carnes Lord in his translation in Strauss, *Xenophon's Socratic Discourse* (Ithaca, 1970), p. 25, supplies, against the evidence of all the MSS, a predicate to govern the subordinate clause which Kritoboulos has begun to express himself in. Juan Gil in his edition of the *Oik.* (Madrid, 1967) favors the emendation of Stephanus, reading ἔτι δέ for the ὅτι δέ of the tradition. Pierre Chantraine in the

Budé text (Paris, 1949) preserves the MSS reading as it should be.

67. 5.20.

68. This is a point stressed by Strauss, *Xenophon's Socratic Discourse*, pp. 159ff. and *passim*, and it is also made by Sandra Novo, *Economia ed Etica nell' Economico di Senofonte* (Turin, 1968), pp. 33-5, 42-3. This distinction made by Xenophon should give more pause than it has to those writers on the *Oik.* who seem content to equate Xenophon and Iskhomakhos and to view the work as some kind of autobiographical account of life at Skillous. For all that it matters for an understanding of the work, Xenophon may have loathed farming, a topic he may have chosen here because it is the topic *par excellence* of didactic literature. In any event Hesiod did not have to be a farmer to write the *Works and Days*; by his own admission he was a shepherd.

69. 12.6, 12.10, 13.4, 14.3, 8.18-22.

70. 11.9, 20.26-9. Iskhomakhos' generosity may have been his own undoing, if he is the same man mentioned in Andokides, *On the Mysteries* 124, and in the fragments of the comedians, Araros 16 and Kratinos 328 (Edmonds). His good nature proved his own undoing, even as Socrates' proved his.

71. 11.3.

72. 11.4-6. Socrates says that in joy at his discovery he *anekupsa*, which is generally translated "heaved a sigh of relief" or *vel sim* but can also mean "to arch the neck high, like a horse."

73. 17.15.

74. 1.1ff.; 6.4.

75. 2.2ff.

76. 7.1-2. *Mem.* 1.1.10.

77. For Socrates' autarchy, cf. *Mem.* 1.2.14, 4.8.11. This is part of the basic outlook of Strauss, *Xenophon's Socrates*, pp. 8-10, who stresses the implications of what Xenophon leaves unsaid at *Mem.* 1.10ff. He maintains, for instance, that when Xenophon says Socrates spent his days in public, he leaves unclear what Socrates did at night; and when Xenophon says he is surprised at the judges' ignorance of what Socrates did in front of everyone, Strauss suggests that Xenophon meant his intelligent readers to wonder about what Socrates did in private and which Xenophon is not surprised the judges did not know. In short what Socrates silently deliberated was not always what Socrates said or did. But this speculation is rather like the questionable critical procedure of wondering what a character in a play does when offstage and unmentioned. Furthermore granting Socrates had another life, it does not follow necessarily that it conflicted with his public one.

78. 1.2.48.

79. 1.6.2ff.

80. 1.6.13.

81. 1.6.14.

82. 1.6.15.

83. Xenophon naturally must have realized that the mind can converse with itself, but it seems indicative of the whole tenor of his understanding of Socrates and the philosophic life that he nowhere stresses this and nowhere offers a definition of *dianoia* like the one Plato provides at *Sophist* 264a or *Theaitetos* 190a. Aristotle NE 10, 1177a28ff, says that the philosopher can contemplate on his own, unlike the brave man who needs a theater for his bravery, and that this constitutes the autarchy of the philosophic life; but he adds that the philosopher can do better if he has fellow-workers, just as earlier in the same work he denies that self-sufficiency means a life of isolation (1, 1097b7 ff.). Xenophon's thought seems to emphasize these latter aspects.

84. *Oik.* 5.1, where, in a chapter which sees the heightening of rhetoric to a visionary level, Socrates says that farming is a pleasure, an increase of what one owns, and an exercise befitting a free man. It goes without saying that Socrates was to Xenophon amongst the blest and the free. In some sense, then, he too was a "farmer." Cf. the comparison made at *Sym.* 8.25 between the devotee of the heavenly love and a man who owns his own field: both do all they can to make the object of their affection increase in value.

85. *Mem.* 1.2.14; 4.6.15.

86. The book in large part concerns Socrates' education of a typical subject, the young know-it-all Euthydemos. It begins with the subverting of Euthydemos' misplaced self-confidence and the invitation to self-knowledge, then progresses to attitudes towards the gods and self-control, and finally to discussions of logical divisions and definitions. This structural principle has also been commented on by Strauss, *Xenophon's Socrates*, pp. 91ff. It should also become clear that the *Mem.* sustains to the end a unified design. For just as Books Two and Three moved in tandem, being concerned with Socrates and others, Books One and Four are intimately concerned with aspects of Socrates himself. The *Mem.* in its very construction is witness to the equilibrium between the individual and the *polis* which Xenophon attempts to establish within it.

87. 4.1.2.

88. 4.2.25-9.

89. 1.7.

90. 4.7.6.

91. 1.6.10. Cf. also *Apol.* 15.

92. *Mem.* 1.3.2-3.

93. 1.1.11-3.

94. 1.2.2-3. Thus, too, the form of the *Mem.* becomes all the more appropriate, since it belonged, as a *logos Sokratikos*, to the realm of mimetic literature (Cf. Aristotle, *Poetics* 1447b9-20) and so had as one object to speak and work upon the reader in just the same way as Socrates' discussions once had worked upon his listeners and fellow interlocutors (cf. Heinrich Maier, *Sokrates* [Tübingen, 1913], p. 38).

95. *Apol.* 3.

96. On the "tragic limitation" of speech, cf. Strauss, *Xenophon's Socratic Discourse*, pp. 176-177.
97. *Apol.* 4.
98. *Apol.* 1. The "big talk" may also be discovered in the first word of the work—Socrates—the only Socratic work of Xenophon which so stresses its chief personality.
99. *Apol.* 13-4, 21.
100. *Kyro.* 7.1.17.
101. *Apol.* 4.
102. *Apol.* 23 (Contrast Plato, *Apology* 38b6-9).
103. Contrast Plato, *Apology*, 40c5ff. It may be taken as a token of the fancy of the *Kyro.* that the dying Cyrus is permitted such a speculation, 8.7.17ff.
104. *Apol.* 16, 27.
105. *Apol.* 14, 32. For a further appreciation of the dimension of envy, chapter five, book fifteen of Augustine's *City of God* may be consulted with profit.
106. *Mem.* 3.9.8.
107. *Mem.* 4.4.4-5.
108. *On Irony*, Part 1, Chapter 1. It is unfortunate that Kierkegaard could see in the irony of Xenophon at most the irony which is the accoutrement of good breeding.

Chapter 3

1. *Kyro.* 1.1.
2. Herodotos 1.108ff. Cf. also C. H. Lehmann-Haupt, "Der Sturz des Kroisos und das historische Element in Xenophons Kyropädie," *Wiener Studien* 47 (1929): 123ff., WS 50 (1932): 152ff.
3. *Kyro.* 1.2.9, 1.2.4.
4. 5.5.5ff., 8.5.20ff., 8.7.6ff.
5. 1.2.3.
6. 1.2.6, and esp. 1.3.17.
7. 1.2.7.
8. 8.3.49.
9. 1.2.15.
10. 1.3.18.
11. 1.3.8ff., 1.4.7ff., 1.4.21.
12. 1.5.8ff. On his deathbed, 8.7.7, he will say that he did not let his fatherland remain an *idiōtēs* amongst the nations of Asia. For his love of money, cf. 8.2.20.
13. 1.5.2ff., 2.4.31-2, 7.5.73.
14. 8.5.24.
15. 7.5.85-6, 8.7.10.
16. For a meditation on this problem, cf. Machiavelli, *Discorsi*, 1.29.2,

1.30.2.

17. Kyro. 8.4.11.

18. 1.4.12-3.

19. The classic presentation is Wilhelm Prinz, *De Xenophontis Cyri Institutione* (Göttingen, 1911). It was adequately refuted by Erwin Scharr, *Xenophons Staats und Gesellschaftsideal und seine Zeit* (Halle, 1919), pp. 25ff.

20. Kyro. 1.2.15.

21. 6.2.11, 4.2.1. (cf. Herodotos 1.69-70, 1.83).

22. It has been thought that mention of Rheomithres and Mithridates at 8.8.4 is an allusion to the Satraps' Revolt of c. 362. But the date of the revolt is in question; cf. the discussion in M.N. Tod, *Greek Historical Inscriptions*, Vol. 2 (Oxford, 1948), Number 145. A date for the *Kyro.*, in the sixties at the earliest, is rendered likely if the great battle of Thymbrara is modelled on Leuktra. Cf. the discussion in J.K. Anderson, *Greek Military Tactics in the Age of Xenophon* (Berkeley, 1970), pp. 165ff. Theoretically no *terminus ante* can be established.

23. Kyro. 3.1.7, 3.1.38.

24. 3.1.25. This idea seems to have become a commonplace in the philosophical tradition and receives its most memorable statement, of course, in Lucretius, 3.79-82.

25. Kyro. 5.2.9-10. Contrast the evil secrecy of the Assyrian, 4.6.4.

26. 3.3.3.

27. 7.1.2-3, 8.5.3.

28. 7.1.22.

29. 2.2.15-6.

30. 2.2.14.

31. 2.4.10.

32. 2.2.13. Cf. also how the charm of the boy Cyrus increases with his increase in modesty and reticence, 1.4.4. He is ever his creator's child.

33. 5.2.18.

34. 2.2.15.

35. Emerson, *Essay on Heroism*. Hilarity was the quality Emerson seems to have admired most in heroes. Cicero also remarks on the humor of Cyrus, mentioning how Xenophon has joined to his hero's highest gravity a singular levity *(comitate)*, Ep. ad Q.Fr. 1.1.23.

36. Kyro. 2.1.21.

37. 2.4.22, 2.4.10, 8.2.2.

38. Cf., e.g., 3.3.62.

39. 2.1.11.

40. 5.3.46-7.

41. 2.3.17.

42. 2.1.17.

43. 2.1.25.

44. 3.3.70.

45. 7.5.76, 8.2.23.

46. 6.4.1.
47. 8.2.5. This text merited the attention of Marx, *Das Kapital*, Part 4 Chapter 14, Section 5, who comments that Xenophon views division of labor as a means to better quality, not to a cheapening in the name of mass production.
48. *Kyro.* 8.1.2, 8.7.13.
49. 3.3.44ff.
50. 3.3.55.
51. 7.2.28.
52. 7.2.29. On Xenophon's changing of the Herodotean tradition in the Cyrus-Croesus encounter, cf. Eckard Lefèvre, "Die Frage nach dem βίος εὐδαίμων. Die Begegnung zwischen Kyros und Kroisos bei Xenophon," *Hermes* 99 (1971): 283ff.
53. *Kyro.* 6.4.9.
54. 7.3.16.
55. 7.1.41ff, 8.5.19.
56. 4.1.24. Cf. also Lefèvre, "Die Frage.," p. 292, for the intimation of Cyrus' divinity by his playing the role for Croesus which had been played in Herodotos by the Oracle at Delphi.
57. Alfred Croiset, *Xénophon, son caractère et son talent* (Paris, 1873), p. 219.
58. The remark of Ben Edwin Perry, *The Ancient Romances* (Berkeley, 1967), p. 178, is worth citing in full: "Parallel to the extension of encomiastic literature from poetry into prose . . . is the extension into prose narrative, in the form of ideal romance, of the artistic methods which had previously been recognized as legitimate only in some kind of ideal poetry, chiefly in epic and in classical 'tragedy' . . ."
59. Xenophon may be said to prefigure from afar the work of modern pyschologists who have developed phases of psychological growth spanning the entire life cycle of man. Cf., in a Freudian context, Erik Erikson, "The Problem of Ego Identity," in *Psychological Issues*, Vol. 1, No. 1, Monograph 1, pp. 101ff.
60. *Kyro.* 7.5.75-6.
61. 1.6.8.
62. 7.5.37-40, 8.7.12. Cyrus, in having to impress a vanquished foe's populace, reverts to the rouged and impressively arrayed model of his grandfather, whose own daughter called his approach to rule more tyrannical than royal, 1.3.18. On the paradoxical union of vast power and constant labor, cf. Pascal, *Pensées* 113 (Brunschvicg), on the Sultan.
63. *Kyro.* 8.1.22.
64. 8.1.1. This analogy of father and good ruler is not original with Xenophon. Sophokles' tyrant Oidipous, for instance, calls his subjects his children (*tekna*, line 1), and, if Aristotle's *Constitution of the Athenians* can be believed, Nikias and Thucydides the son of Melesias maintained a fatherly attitude in their command (chapter 28).
65. Cf. the case of the teacher executed by Tigranes' father whose

lessons, however, enable Tigranes to save his father's life before Cyrus, 3.1.14ff.

66. 3.3.12, 8.4.18-9, Sym. 3.10.

67. Machiavelli, *Discorsi* 2.13.1, notes this well but fails to make clear that Cyrus' deception is practiced against foes, not his own people. As for Kyaxares, it was more a case of coddling than confounding.

68. Cf. Aristotle's criticism of his teacher in *On Kingship* (Rose, *Fragments*, 646-647) that philosophy might even be a hindrance to a governor, but that governors should listen to philosophers and be receptive to their advice.

69. *Kyro.* 8.1.8, 8.8.5.

70. The clear necessity for a balancing falling action to complement the first chapter of the *Kyro.* should have precluded the theory that Xenophon added the last chapter after the rest of the *Kyro.* was already completed. It should also be evident that Xenophon need not have undergone some change of heart about the Persians which made him add the last chapter as a corrective to his "earlier" views. The whole work is a fantasy whose historical untruth Xenophon knew full well from the beginning. Needless to say he had himself known Persian perfidy firsthand as early as 401, and unless someone is prepared to date the *Kyro.* before then, it is beside the point to wonder what alleged change or historical event brought about the work's bitter conclusion.

71. *Kyro.* 7.5.86. He had, by the way, forgotten the implicit lesson of those who deserted to his side from the Assyrian's, like Gadatas and Gobryas: they had been loyal to the Assyrian's father, but the insolence of the son and successor alienated them.

72. Cf. Eduard Schwartz, *Fünf Vorträge über den grieschischen Roman* (Berlin, 1896), p. 54; Ivo Bruns, *Das literarische Porträt der Griechen* (Berlin, 1896), p. 416.

73. *Kyro.* 1.6.46.

74. On this, cf. Machiavelli, *Discorsi* 1.11.5-6.

75. *Noctes Atticae* 14.3.3. Cf. the wisecrack at Plato, *Laws* 695a.

76. *Sym.* 8.39, *Mem.* 4.2.2, 2.6.13.

Chapter 4

1. *Kyro.* 7.5.58.
2. *Mem.* 4.6.12.
3. *Hi.* 1.1.
4. 1.8.
5. 1.9.
6. He uses $eg\bar{o}$ six times in the first chapter alone.
7. Cf., e.g., 1.35, 2.15, 4.1, 6.2.
8. 4.1.
9. 3.3.

10. 3.8. Although the argument develops naturally here according to its own themes, scholars may not be wrong to see in this passage an allusion to events in the Thessalian tyranny which occured in 358 (cf. Hell. 6.4.33-7) and thus to secure a terminus for the composition of the dialogue. Cf. Jean Hatzfeld, "Note sur la date et l'objet du Hiéron," Revue des Etudes Grecques 59 (1946): 54ff., and G.J.D. Aalders, "The Date and Intention of Xenophon's Hiero," Mnemosyne 6 (1953): series four, pp. 208ff. Of course Xenophon could have made the same observation from his knowledge of the Corinthian tyranny of Periandros.

11. Hi. 2.7ff.
12. 5.1ff.
13. 1.32-3.
14. Oik. 21.12.
15. Hi. 1.31.
16. 1.1, 2.5.
17. Chapters three through six are almost entirely a monologue.
18. 6.4. Cf. the truthful, though unaware, humor of the present and future tyrant of the Sym., Kharmides, who said that he liked to live dangerously (4.34).
19. Hi. 6.9. ὑπέρευ is ironic. Marchant's Loeb translation does not make this clear ("Excellent words in part, I grant") and Luccioni's is tout à fait wrong: "Tu as tout à fait raison à mon avis" (edition of the Hi., with trans., [Paris, 1948], ad loc.)
20. Leo Strauss, On Tyranny (London, 1963), p. 48, seems to think the former, for he writes that "to describe in one sentence the art employed by Xenophon in the first part of the Hiero, we may say that by choosing a conversational setting in which the strongest possible indictment of tyranny becomes possible, he intimates the limited validity of that indictment."
21. Hi. 1.4, 1.8.
22. Hell. 2.3.1ff.
23. Hi. 7.11.
24. 7.13.
25. 8.1.
26. Cf. the remark of Luccioni, ed. of Hiero, p. 24, who goes a bit too far but realizes the difference in the nature of the discussion when he says that Xenophon basically has in mind a transformation of tyranny into royalty.
27. Mem. 2.1.1ff.
28. Hi. 8.3ff., 11.1ff.
29. 8.5. Cf. Hesiod, Theogony 80ff. where, significanly, the reference is to kings.
30. Hi. 10.1ff., esp. 10.8.
31. 11.6. This quietly rebuts Hiero at 4.6, where he had argued that the tyrant, like the athlete, is not happy when he beats laymen but is mortified when he is bested by his own peers. Hiero, in other words,

suppressed the positive: the tyrant is happy when he is superior to his peers.

32. 11.7-8. Cf. M.N. Tod, *Greek Historical Inscriptions*, Vol. 2 (Oxford, 1948), Number 136, for a discussion of Dionysios I's victory in the tragic contest at the Lenaia in 367. Jason competed at the Pythian Games (*Hell.* 6.4.30). Hiero, of course, was paid the compliment of Pindaric odes for his prowess in sport.

33. *Hi.* 11.11.

34. 11.13-4.

35. Strauss, *On Tyranny*, p. 60.

36. *Mem.* 3.5.16, *Sym.* 8.35 and 39.

37. Cf. Jean Luccioni, *Les idées politiques et sociales de Xénophon* (Paris, 1947), p. 163; Edouard Delebecque, "Sur la date et l'objet de l'Economique," *Revue des Études Grecques* 64 (1951): p. 27; Leo Strauss, *Xenophon's Socratic Discourse* (Ithaca, N.Y., 1970), pp. 200-2.

38. *Oik.* 14.4-8.

39. *Mem.* 3.5.14-5.

40. Cf. the remark of Wilhelm Prinz, *De Xenophontis Cyri Institutione* (Göttingen, 1911), p. 18.

41. François Ollier, edition of the *CofL* with commentary (Lyons, 1934), ad 11.10.

42. Luccioni, *Les idées*, p. 162.

43. Thus Ollier, ed. of *CofL*, who prints the chapter last, and K.M.T. Chrimes, *The Res Publica Lacedaemoniorum Ascribed to Xenophon* (Manchester, 1948), p. 8, who puts forth the singular theory, in a monograph filled with singular theories, that the fourteenth chapter should be placed not last but first. Also, for a final position, Hans Breitenbach, "Xenophon," article in Pauly-Wissowa-Kroll, *Realencyclopädie der Altertumswissenschaft*, Vol. 18, second series, col. 1751.

44. Thus, typically, Delebecque, *Essai sur la vie de Xénophon* (Paris, 1957), pp. 194-5, 329; also Luccioni, *Les idées*, p. 171. For a sensible criticism of such views, cf. Arnaldo Momigliano, "Per l'Unità Logica della Lacedaimonion Politeia," in his *Terzo Contributo* (Rome, 1966), pp. 341-5.

45. Cf. Prinz, *De Xenophontis*, p. 74, note 15, and J.D. Denniston, *Greek Prose Style* (Oxford, 1952), p. 44, both of whom point out that no classical author would put what he wanted to keep from attention in prominent positions like the beginning or the end of a piece.

46. This is the approach taken, though from a different angle, by Leo Strauss, "The Spirit of Sparta or the Taste of Xenophon," *Social Research* 6 (1939): 502ff. For a presentation of the received tradition—or the usual bromides—Eugène Napoleon Tigerstedt, *The Legend of Sparta in Classical Antiquity* (Stockholm, 1965), pp. 159ff., may conveniently be consulted. Lest it be objected that Xenophon had his own sons educated in Sparta, it should be pointed out that this information derives from a notice in Diokles reported by Diogenes Laertios (2.54). Diokles was hardly Xenophon's contemporary; he seems, moreover, to have been rather an admirer of Antisthenes. Diokles may have invented a story about Xenophon's sons

to suit his own disposition and his own purposes or he may have taken the item from another work with a similar bent. In any case the story must be viewed cautiously, since Xenophon himself says nothing about his sons' boarding in Sparta but does show them living with him at Skillous (*Anab.* 5.3.10).

47. *CofL* 1.6-7.
48. 1.5.
49. 2.8. For the important distinction Lykourgos failed to make, cf. *Kyro.* 8.1.31 (whether or not the text is to be retained).
50. *CofL* 7.1-5.
51. 7.6.
52. 1.9.
53. 5.3.
54. 10.4, 10.7.
55. 8.5.
56. Cf. Polybios' report (10.2.9-13) of how the astute Roman politician Scipio Aemilianus consciously took a lesson from Lykourgos in capitalizing on religious scruples.
57. *CofL.* 12.10-11.
58. 12.11.
59. 3.1, 4.7.
60. 12.7.
61. Note the difficulties encountered by Xenophon's ideal Persians when they experimented once in this fashion: *Kyro.* 1.6.31-4.
62. *CofL* 4.6. Note also that guards in the army on campaign were stationed around the armory to watch out for friends, not for enemies: 12.2.
63. 1.7-10. The contemporaries of Xenophon had witnessed the dispute over succession to the Spartan throne which arose because of the doubtful paternity of Leotykhidas: *Hell.* 3.3.1ff.
64. *CofL* 3.5.
65. 3.4.
66. Cf. Ribbeck, "Über den Begriff des εἴρων," *Rheinisches Museum* 31 (1876): 386, apropos of the *Rhetorica ad Alexandrum* 1441b24. The technique is not peculiar to Greek literature. Readers of Catullus have enjoyed its use.
67. *Panathenaikos* 233ff. Cf. the comments in general of Jacqueline de Romilly, *Histoire et raison chez Thucydide* (Paris, 1956), pp. 103-4.
68. Cf. the perceptive remark of Strauss, "The Spirit of Sparta," p. 531: "The treatise of Xenophon is, then, a remarkable document of Attic taste: it represents a higher type of comic speech than does the classical comedy. Yet, just as there is no jest without underlying seriousness, there is no good taste which is not something more than taste. The true name of that taste which permeates Xenophon's writings is, not education, but philosophy." To argue that Xenophon could not have written such a tract while the guest of a Spartan king (Delebecque, *La vie,* p. 194) may be true but begs the question. There is no conclusive proof that the treatise was written during Xenophon's stay at Skillous. Furthermore the

perception of a decline in Sparta as expressed in the fourteenth chapter has usually been taken to indicate a date of 378, when Sparta's high-handed actions in Thebes provoked a new alliance of opponents, who eventually brought Sparta low. But the decline, as Xenophon presents it, could suit Sparta in the 360s no less, and many Greeks, indeed Peloponnesians, were more active in the sixties in their attempts to destroy Spartan leadership. This is not sufficiently appreciated by Breitenbach, "Xenophon" col. 1752, who favors a date just at the time of Leuktra, 371.

69. CofL. 9.6.

70. Cf., e.g., 2.1, 2.14, 5.5, 6.1, 6.4, 7.1, etc. Ollier has called the CofL a piece of propaganda for Sparta but wonders why Xenophon so berates other cities rather than attempts to persuade them. His solution is as labored as it is unconvincing: it is the spirit of hard feeling which overtook Xenophon because of his exile. Cf. Ollier's Le Mirage Spartiate (Paris, 1933), p. 401.

71. Aristotle's thought on Sparta is similar: cf. Politics, 2.9.

72. CofL. 15.1.

73. 13.11, 15.4-5.

74. 15.6.

75. Ibid.

76. 15.8.

77. 8.4.

78. Cf. Diels, Fragmente der Vorsokratiker, Vol. 2, Number 88, frgs. 6, 32-7, and Strauss, "The Spirit of Sparta," pp. 528-9. Hell. 2.3-4.

79. CofL 15.9.

Chapter 5

1. Hell. 3.3.3, 5.4.58.

2. On the principles of encomiastic writing, cf. Ivo Bruns, Das literarische Porträt der Griechen (Berlin, 1896), p. 127; also Arnaldo Dante Momigliano, The Development of Greek Biography (Cambridge, Mass., 1971), pp. 49-52. On the style of the Ages., cf. Walter Seyfert, De Xenophontis Agesilao Quaestionis (Göttingen, 1909) and Alfonsus Opitz, Quaestiones Xenophonteae: de Hellenicorum atque Agesilai necessitudine (Breslau, 1913).

3. Hell. 4.1.34.

4. On Xenophon's return to Athens, cf. Chapter Seven.

5. Cf. Plato, Menexenos 237a. Also, Rhetorica ad Alexandrum 1440b 15ff.

6. Ages. 1.4.

7. Ibid.

8. 7.1.

9. 1.7-8, 1.36.

10. 4.5.

11. 5.3.
12. 8.6, 9.3-5, 11.11-2.
13. 8.1.
14. 1.38. Cf. also 7.3. for Agesilaos' fatherly attitude towards political opponents.
15. 2.13.
16. 1.21.
17. 11.3.
18. 8.8.
19. 1.36.
20. 2.16.
21. 9.5.
22. 9.1-2.
23. 9.1.
24. 1.6, 3.1.
25. 10.2.
26. 1.1.
27. 10.1.
28. 2.7-8.
29. 7.5.
30. This may explain Xenophon's insistence that he is in no way writing a threnody, even though he is writing about a dead man: 10.3. For the development of the encomium and biography out of the funeral song, cf. Friedrich Leo, *Die griechische-römische Biographie nach ihrer literarischen Form* (Leipzig, 1901), p. 87.
31. *Anab.* 3.1.5.
32. 3.1.5-7.
33. 2.6.16.
34. 1.9.5-6.
35. 1.9.16-9.
36. 1.9.1.
37. 1.9.13.
38. Contrast Socrates' advice at *Mem.* 2.3. Cyrus would also have done well to have learned the lesson taught his great namesake at *Kyro.* 1.3.16-7 where a big boy finds he is not entitled to take a small boy's tunic, which was too large for its owner, and to substitute his own, which was too small for him, even though both boys would thus wind up with a properly fitting garment.
39. *Anab.* 1.4.12.
40. 6.4.8.
41. *Ibid.*; also 1.4.9.
42. 1.3.2ff., 2.6.7-9.
43. 1.4.7ff.
44. 1.3.17ff.
45. 1.5.7-8.
46. 2.3.11, 3.4.47-8, 4.4.12.

47. 1.5.8.
48. 1.7.20.
49. 1.8.2.
50. 1.8.26ff.; cf. also 1.7.9.
51. 1.8.29.
52. 1.7.3.
53. 1.9.31, 2.5.35.
54. 2.1.5, 2.1.9.
55. 2.1.10-1.
56. 2.1.18-9.
57. 2.1.13.
58. 2.4.4.
59. 2.4.19.
60. 2.5.3ff.
61. 2.5.16ff., esp. 2.5.22.
62. 3.1.2 with its sobering echo of their previous boast about being "at the doors of the King."
63. 3.1.3.
64. 3.1.31.
65. 3.1.38.
66. 3.2.30.
67. Cf. esp. Gerald Nussbaum, "The Captains of the Ten Thousand," *Classica et Mediaevalia* 20 (1959): 16ff., and *The Ten Thousand: A Study in Social Organization and Action in Xenophon's Anabasis* (Leiden, 1967).
68. Anab. 3.3.15ff.
69. On the nature of this difference in which Xenophon may see a typical difference between Spartans and Athenians, cf. Nussbaum, *The Ten Thousand*, p. 120.
70. Anab. 4.3.10, 7.6.38.
71. 3.2.25.
72. 4.8.25.
73. 5.1.4.
74. 5.1.2.
75. 5.1.14.
76. 5.1.7,8,9,11,12. Paul Masqueray in the Budé *Anab.*, note complémentaire *ad* 5.1.12 misinterprets this repetition as an example of Xenophon's inexhaustible loquacity.
77. 5.4.15ff.
78. 5.7.13ff.
79. 5.7.26.
80. 6.4.23, 6.2.13-4, 7.2.2.
81. 6.2.1ff., 7.1.15ff. At Kerasos the force numbered 8600 (5.3.3); at 7.7.23. Xenophon commands 6000.
82. 6.3.24-5.
83. 5.8.13.
84. 5.6.15-6.

85. 6.6.16.
86. 6.1.20.
87. 7.7.41.
88. 7.6.38.
89. 5.8.25-6.
90. 6.1.21.
91. 7.6.11.
92. 7.8.3. Cf. also the hard-nosed assessment of Seuthes at 7.6.4: because Xenophon was too concerned for the soldiers, he was not as well off as he might have been.
93. Félix Dürrbach, "L'Apologie de Xénophon," *Revue des Études Grecques* 6 (1893): 346ff.
94. On Themistogenes, cf. *Hell.* 3.1.2 and for a discussion of his identity, cf. Hans Breitenbach, "Xenophon," article in Pauly-Wissowa *Realencyclopädie der Altertumswissenschaft*, Vol. 18, second series, col. 1644; Plutarch *De gloria Atheniensium* 1. For a possible deeper motivation, cf. the concluding remarks of the present chapter.
95. On the *Tendenzproblem*, cf. Breitenbach, "Xenophon", col. 1644ff. and Alfred Körte, "Die Tendenz von Xenophons Anabasis," *Neue Jahrbücher* 49 (1922): 15ff.
96. For the remains of Sophainetos, cf. Jacoby, *Fragmente der Griechischen Historiker* II B 107.
97. Suggestions for the date of the *Anabasis* range from the mid-380s to the 360s.
98. For an example of such antipathy, cf. Philip Merlan, "Isokrates, Aristotle, and Alexander the Great," *Historia* 3 (1954): 60ff. Note also the remarks of Hartmut Erbse, "Xenophons Anabasis," *Gymnasium* 73 (1966): pp. 503-4. The attempt by Münschner, "Xenophon in der griechischrömischen Literatur," *Philologus*, Supplement 13 (1920): 25-7, to establish important use of Xenophon by Ephoros and Theopompos (also an Isokratean pupil) is hardly convincing.
99. Not that Diodoros' source, Ephoros, was always historically enlightened in neglecting Xenophon. For example, in using Ktesias he would have erred in following that writer's account of Klearkhos as a victim of the army's insistence in going to see Tissaphernes (Jacoby III C 688, frg. 27) rather than preserving the *Anab.*'s picture of Klearkhos' going on his own initiative (2.5.24ff.). For Ktesias, as Plutarch makes clear (*Artaxerxes* 13.4), was a devoted admirer of the Spartan and would naturally have done everything to cover up his foolish shortcomings.
100. *Anab.* 1.8.26-7.
101. 3.4.7-12.
102. 4.8.20, 5.4.34, 6.4.6, 6.6.1-2.
103. Cf. Diodoros 14.30, where similar accounts of the honey and Mossynoiki episodes are given. Xenophon's accuracy has also had its supporters, among whom are Breitenbach, "Xenophon," col. 1647ff., Erbse, "Xenophons Anabasis," pp. 485ff., and J. Roy, "Xenophon's Ana-

basis: The Command of the Rearguard in Books 3 and 4," *Phoenix* 22 (1968): 158-9, and Roy, "Xenophon's Evidence for the Anabasis," *Athenaeum* 46 (1968): 37ff.

104. Breitenbach, "Xenophon," col. 1579ff., amongst others, considers the *Anab.* and the *Hell.* under the same critical heading. He is, however, aware of the difficulty of determining the genre of the *Anab.* and is more on the right track in suggesting a connection with the work of Ion of Chios. In other words the *Anab.* more properly belongs to the geographical literature and the literature of travel tradition which goes back to Herodotos and, ultimately, to Homer. More light may be put on this question by recalling the clear distinction made by Kallisthenes between his own *Hellenika* and his account of Alexander's march up-country and by recognizing the willingness of someone as seemingly sober as Nearkhos to let fancy play with the facts of his own journey's narrative, not to mention the similar and even greater disposition of Onesikritos to do likewise in a work which may have been modelled on the *Anab.* (On this, cf. Lionel Pearson, *The Lost Histories of Alexander the Great* [American Philological Assoc., 1960], pp. 87ff., where, it must be confessed, the argument is strained, although the influence of Xenophon is undeniable on Onesikritos, if not as precise as Pearson would make it.) The *Anab.*, that is, may never have been expected to display the care for accuracy which might be demanded of a straight history like the *Hell.*, where, in fact, Xenophon does make an effort to sift through, or at least present, different accounts of one event. Cf. Chapter Six, note 135. This contrast in approach may also be appreciated by comparing the different way (which has nothing to do with a different personality or ability) Thucydides recounts, in an undeniably "historical" account (7.75ff.), the retreat of an army explicitly likened to a city, the retreating Athenians after Syracuse. Gibbon, who was of course no slouch when it came to the facts, was perhaps more aware than many since have been of the special nature of the *Anab.* He calls it "original and authentic" and points out, without critical tone, that "Xenophon's memory, perhaps many years after the expedition, has sometimes betrayed him" (*Decline and Fall*, chapter 24, at note 49 in the Bury ed.).

105. *Anab.* 3.2.25, 5.1.2. The deliberateness of the Lotus Eaters reference may perhaps be ascertained by recognizing that this is one of the very few reminiscences of this Homeric scene in Greek literature. Cf. Sir Denys Page, *Folktales in Homer's Odyssey* (Cambridge, Mass., 1973: The 1972 Jackson Lectures), pp. 6-7.

106. *Anab.* 7.8.24.

107. 6.2.15, 7.6.44.

108. 3.1.12.

109. 5.3.8-13.

110. Cf. *Panegyrikos* 149 and *Anab.* 2.4.4: καὶ τελευτῶντες ὑπ'αὐτοῖς τοῖς βασιλείοις καταγέλαστοι γεγόνασιν—ὡς ἡμεῖς τοσοίδε ὄντες ἐνικῶμεν τὸν βασιλέα ἐπὶ ταῖς θύραις αὐτοῦ καὶ καταγελάσαντες ἀπήλθομεν.

Basing his argument on this supposed borrowing by Isokrates, Alfred Kappelmacher, "Zur Abfassungszeit von Xenophons Anabasis," *Anzeiger der Akademie der Wissenschaft in Wien* 60 (1923): 15ff., held that the *Anab.* had to be dated before the completion of the Isokrates speech in 380. His date is as weak as his alleged allusion. (It is, of course, logically possible, if hardly probable, that Xenophon could be the imitator and not the imitated.) Another parallel between *Panegyrikos* 146 and *Anab.* 7.7.23 concerning the numbers on the expedition is equally inconclusive. For though Xenophon is the only source still preserved which contains the same figure as Isokrates, it need not have been the only source available to Isokrates in his time. He could have taken it from Sophainetos. Those who also favor an early date because the narrative of Xenophon is so fresh that it must have been written soon after the experiences described do not give Xenophon's literary ability sufficient credit. Unfortunately, however, a firm late date for the *Anab.* is not provided by the text. The uses of past tenses in the description of life at Skillous may be epistolary; the reference to Spartan control of Greek cities at 6.6.9 could apply anytime after 395, and the connection with the obituaries of the generals and Isokrates' *Evagoras* are slender and abstruse.

111. Cf. *Hell.* 3.2.18, 3.4.2, 6.1.12.
112. *Anab.* 1.5.9.
113. Diogenes Laertios 2.58.

Chapter 6

1. George Grote, *History of Greece*, Vol. 8 (1856 ed.), p. 155, note 1. P. Defosse, "A propos du début insolite des *Helléniques*," *Revue Belge* 46 (1968): 5ff., argues unconvincingly for a lacuna at the start of the work in which Xenophon would have made mention of a few details to make the connection with Thuc. 8 more neat. But even he admits that as the *Hell.* now stands a knowledge of Thuc. 8 is essential, and the details he misses may have been thought inconsequential by Xenophon on the principle enunciated at *Hell.* 4.8.1. The use of δέ will of course present no problem: it is connective to the end of Thuc. Of Defosse's argument that Xenophon must have introduced himself in the alleged lacuna so that no one could get the wrong idea that Thuc. was still the author of these war events, the less said the better.

2. B.G. Niebuhr, "Über Xenophons Hellenika," *Rheinisches Museum* 1 (1827): 194ff. Also in *Kleine Schriften*, Vol. 1 (Bonn, 1828), pp. 464ff.

3. The matter has been laid to rest by Paul Cloché, "Les Helléniques de Xénophon et Lacédémone," *Revue des Etudes Anciennes* 46 (1944): 12ff.

4. *Hell.* 2.4.43. Niebuhr, "Über Xenophons Hellenika," p. 195/466. For a similar position cf. G.E. Underhill, *A Commentary on Xenophon's Hellenika* (Oxford, 1900), ad loc.

5. Pointed out by Hans Baden, *Untersuchungen zur Einheit der Hellenika Xenophons* (Hamburg, 1966), p. 31.

6. The method was suggested by W. Dittenberger, "Sprachliche Kriterien für die Chronologie der Platonischen Dialoge," *Hermes* 16 (1881): pp. 321-45.

7. Eduard Schwartz, "Quellenuntersuchungen zur griechischen Geschichte," *Rheinisches Museum* 44 (1889): 184-5. Also in *Gesammelte Schriften*, Vol. 2 (Berlin, 1956), pp. 163-4.

8. Thus the phrase describing Koroneia as a battle "like none other in my time" (*Hell.* 4.3.16) was thought to be incompatible with a time of composition after Leuktra or Mantineia, certainly greater battles than Koroneia. But as Jean Hatzfeld has shown, "Notes sur la composition des Helléniques," *Revue de Philologie* 4 (1930): 123, the words refer not to the size or importance of the battle but to the nature of its progress. Klaus Bringman, "Xenophons Hellenika und Agesilaos," *Gymnasium* 78 (1971): 231-2, argues against this interpretation by pointing out that military historians consider Koroneia a classic textbook battle and that it therefore ought not to be thought unique. This misses Xenophon's point, which is not so much the manoeuvres of the battle as it is Agesilaos' heroic response to their development. Finally it should not go unnoticed that Xenophon felt no unease at using exactly the same phrase in the *Agesilaos* (2.9), a work which must be dated after Leuktra and Mantineia.

9. An inscription was found recording a dedication by the exiled Spartan king Pausanias to his son Agesipolis after the latter's death in 381/80. Cf. M.N.Tod, *Greek Historical Inscriptions*, Vol. 2 (Oxford, 1948), No. 120. This discovery proved untenable the view that Xenophon concluded his narrative at one time at 5.1.31 (the Peace of Antalkidas, 387/86). For Xenophon knew of Pausanias' death—which clearly had to postdate the 381 inscription—and had recorded it not after 5.1.31 but at the conclusion of Book 3. Unfortunate and untypical is the response to this made by Gaetano De Sanctis in "La genesi delle Elleniche di Senofonte," *Annali della R. Scuola Normale Superiore di Pisa: Lettere, storia e filosofia*, 1 (1932): 27-8. For to argue that Xenophon could simply have gone back to Book 3 and added the information about Pausanias' death is to multiply hypotheses when they should be kept to a minimum.

10. Baden, *Untersuchungen*, and W.P. Henry, *Greek Historical Writing* (Chicago, 1966).

11. The event in question is the death of Alexander of Pherai, *Hell.* 6.4.37. Since this is narrated in what Xenophon admits to be a digression from the main account (though not irrelevant to it), it is also possible that the bulk of the *Hell.* was under way or nearing completion by 358, in other words, that composition could extend not over the decades some have assumed or during the years 358-c.354, but over the few years immediately after Mantineia, that is, 361-c.358/7.

12. Marta Sordi, "I caratteri dell'opera storiographica di Senofonte nelle Elleniche," Part 2, *Athenaeum* 29 (1951): 340, who notes the non-

historical nature of many of Xenophon's works.

13. Christopher Ehrhardt, "Xenophon and Diodoros on Aegospotami," Phoenix 24 (1970): 228.

14. Léopold Gautier, La langue de Xénophon (Geneva, 1911), p. 133. This fact is neglected by Sordi, who suggests, "I caratteri dell'opera storigraphica . . ." Part 1, Athenaeum 28 (1950), pp. 3ff., that Books 3 and 4 (down to 4.8) of the Hell. are an addition made by Xenophon to an otherwise unified account of the history in order to complete his narrative in the Anab. More important she has not recognized that the Anab. is different in scope and aim from the Hell.

15. This is the astute observation of Diogenes Laertios in his life of Xenophon at 2.48 (where φιλοσόφων is to be construed with πρῶτος, not, as the Loeb translator does, with ἱστορίαν).

16. On this, cf., amongst others, John Finley, Four Stages of Greek Thought (Stanford, 1966), p. 70.

17. An approach taken by Henry, Greek Historical Writing, p. 45. On the recurring patterns of typically Xenophontic topoi throughout the Hell., cf. Baden, Untersuchungen zur Einheit der Hellenika Xenophons, pp. 68ff., and Peter Krafft, "Vier Beispiele des Xenophontischen in Xenophons Hellenika," Rheinisches Museum 110 (1967), pp. 103ff.

18. As is done by many, amongst whom is Hatzfeld, "Notes sur la composition des Helléniques," pp. 124 and 216. Hatzfeld further claims that the act of completing Thucydides is consummated, not with the destruction of Athens' Long Walls (Hell. 2.2.23), but with the conclusion of Lysander's Samian campaign (2.3.9). This ignores the express words of Thucydides at 5.26.1 of his history. Delebecque's belief in Essai sur la vie de Xénophon (Paris, 1957), pp. 39ff., esp. 52-3, that Thucydides took on the young Xenophon as a secretary in the last decade of the fifth century to aid in the completion of his history and that the bulk of the first two books of the Hell. dates therefore from the years preceding Xenophon's departure from Athens may still find favor with some. Others will consider it pure fantasy.

19. Hell. 2.2.23.

20. 2.3.1-5, reading with the Oxford text of Marchant against the deletion of section 5 in Hatzfeld's Budé text. This section is within the body of the chapter and cannot be so readily classed with the brief annalistic entries of Sicilian affairs which conclude year accounts elsewhere in the first two books. On the problem of interpolations of modes of dating in the first two books in general, cf. Antony Raubitschek, "Die sogenannten Interpolationen in den ersten beiden Büchern von Xenophons Griechischer Geschichte," Akten des VI. Internationales Kongresses für Griechische und Lateinische Epigraphik, Munich, 1972 (Vestigia 17), pp. 315-25, who argues that the citations of archon and ephor years and the rest are original with Xenophon and consistent with a chronology for the events of this part of the War. But he must assume more than a year of inactivity during the rebuilding of the Peloponnesian fleet in 410, when Xenophon

implies something more like two months (1.1.24); he must put off Thrasyllos' expedition by a year, when the account itself suggests promptness (1.1.8 with 1.1.34, rounding off the chapter nicely); and he simply denies Xenophon's explicit statement of a new year beginning at 1.4.2. On these last two points, as well as Raubitschek's confusion about the chronology of Lysander's taking of Samos, cf. the just rebuttal of Detleff Lotze, "War Xenophon selbst der Interpolator seiner Hellenika I-II?" *Philologus* 118 (1974): 215ff. On the ommissions of events leading up to the Thirty, cf. Hatzfeld's *note complémentaire* in the Budé text at 2.3.1. Also Underhill, *A Commentary*, ad loc.

21. *Hell.* 7.5.27.
22. 7.5.26
23. 3.4.12ff., 2.1.24ff.
24. 1.6.36ff., 4.3.13ff.
25. 4.3.14.
26. 3.4.11.
27. 5.4.13.
28. 1.6.14-5.
29. 2.1.32.
30. *Ibid.*
31. 3.5.12-3.
32. 3.5.12, 3.2.21-3.
33. 3.4.5.
34. 3.4.3-4.
35. 4.2.8.
36. *Ages.* 2.1.
37. *Hell.* 5.2.20.
38. 4.6.1ff.
39. 5.2.7.
40. 5.2.32.
41. 5.4.32.
42. 6.3.8.
43. 6.3.9.
44. *Democracy in America*, Part I, Chapter 18, "What are the chances of the duration of the American union?" Cf. also the remarks of K.J. Dover, *Greek Popular Morality* (Berkeley, 1974), pp. 310 ff., on the congruence of vocabulary employed vis-à-vis interpersonal and interstate relations in Greek thought.
45. *Hell.* 2.3.16. Cf. also 2.4.10.
46. 2.3.34.
47. 2.3.50ff.
48. 2.3.35, 1.7.4-6.
49. 2.3.41.
50. For a different view of these speeches, cf. Stephen Usher, "Xenophon, Critias and Theramenes," *Journal of Hellenic Studies* 88 (1968): 130ff.

51. *Hell.* 7.1.44ff.
52. 7.1.46.
53. 7.3.1-3.
54. 7.3.5, 7.3.12.
55. 6.4.28.
56. 6.1.6, 6.1.15-6.
57. This has been commented on by, among others, Hans Breitenbach, *Historiographische Anschauungsformen Xenophons* (Basel, 1950), pp. 60ff.
58. *Hell.* 6.4.29. It is noteworthy that Agesilaos does not receive this honor.
59. 6.4.20ff., esp. 6.4.25.
60. 6.4.32.
61. 1.6.15, 1.6.33.
62. 1.5.11-2, 1.5.16-7.
63. 1.4.12ff., 1.4.20. It should not be assumed, as it often is, that Xenophon was an admirer of Alkibiades just because he recounts at length the reactions of those glad to have Alkibiades back but only mentions briefly the thoughts of the opposition. His narrative here is probably guided by his intention to show all the more how great the fickleness of the Athenians was. His own attitude was more akin to Thucydides': he could admire Alkibiades' mental ability but loathe his totally amoral self-seeking. Alkibiades thus suggests a parallel in the *Hellenika* with Jason. Also, n.b. *Mem.* 1.2.14, where Xenophon couples Alkibiades with Kritias as the two Athenians most addicted to *philotimia.*
64. *Hell.* 1.1.26ff.
65. 3.5.5.
66. 3.5.24.
67. 4.3.1, 4.3.9-10.
68. 4.4.17, 4.5.11ff.
69. 5.3.6.
70. 3.4.29.
71. 1.6.4.
72. 5.4.25ff.
73. 4.1.40.
74. 4.8.24. For another Spartan failure to pursue its own interest cf. 7.1.17.
75. For the connection of war and orgē, cf. *Mem.* 2.6.21.
76. *Hell.* 3.5.5, 3.2.21. The pretenses of this campaign are further undercut by Xenophon's recounting how the leader of Sparta's Elean partisans was a man who could measure his money, rather vulgarly, "by the bushel," while the leader of the opposition, when thought to have been slain, was discovered actually alive but asleep in a drunken stupor. His supporters are described as hovering around him like bees around their queen, while the rest of the Peloponnesos hovers over the fray and finally enters into it because it was proving to be a "gravy train."

77. 3.5.23.
78. 3.5.25. The fate of Pausanias is to be contrasted with the outcome for those who made a similar decision after Leuktra, 6.4.14ff.
79. 5.3.5-6.
80. 5.2.28.
81. 2.1.26.
82. 7.1.24.
83. 7.4.3. Passion of a sexual nature is also shown to subvert chances for success: cf. 5.4.56-7 for the account of Alketas' negligence at Oreon because of a beautiful boy.
84. 1.7.6.
85. 1.7.6-11.
86. 1.7.33.
87. 1.7.5, 1.7.12-5.
88. 2.2.3.
89. 2.2.10.
90. 5.4.24.
91. 3.1.8. Cf. also the incident at Byzantium during the Peloponnesian War at 1.3.19.
92. 3.1.9.
93. 3.1.10ff., esp. 3.1.22.
94. 3.3.5.
95. 3.3.11.
96. *Ibid.*
97. 2.4.41.
98. 3.5.9-10, 3.5.14. On the motives, cf. 3.5.2-3 and esp. 3.5.12 where the Thebans' anger at lost power, honor, and wealth belies their righteous indignation at Sparta's *pleonexia* (3.5.15). Worth noting also is how Thrasyboulos, though agreeing with his fellow Athenians' vote for war, sets the Thebans straight about who is doing whom a favor. (3.5.16).
99. 3.5.8.
100. 5.2.35-6.
101. 7.1.33.
102. 6.5.23-4, 7.1.16.
103. 7.1.42. For a similarly successful policy based upon recognition of local independence and legal observances, cf. 4.8.1 (Konon) and 5.4.64 (Timotheos).
104. 7.5.8ff.
105. 7.5.19.
106. 7.5.18.
107. 7.1.22ff., 7.1.43.
108. 7.5.18.
109. Cf. Plutarch, *Pelopidas* 2, on the danger for cities of leading citizens' personal ambition for honor (apropos of Kallikratidas).
110. *Hell.* 7.5.19.
111. Henry also takes this view, *Greek Historical Writing*, pp. 200-1.

112. Hell. 7.5.8.
113. 7.4.32.
114. 6.4.2-3, and even though Xenophon was fully aware of how Kleombrotos' decision was influenced by the nagging sense of his past failures, 6.4.5. For a recent attempt to exonerate the leadership of Kleombrotos, cf. G.L. Cawkwell, "Epameinondas and Thebes," Classical Quarterly 22 (1972): esp. p. 263. He argues that Xenophon puts the blame for Leuktra on the Spartan king, but that in fact Kleombrotos had done all that could be expected. Spartanism just could not surpass Theban genius. Yet Xenophon's account would not seem to be far different from this very assessment. For Xenophon does not minimize Kleombrotos' accomplishments in troop movements prior to Leuktra (6.4.3-4), and he certainly does not blame Kleombrotos for Sparta's inadequate cavalry in a battle where cavalry would be so crucial (6.4.10-2). The fault, that is, in tactics and preparedness was more Sparta's than Sparta's king's.
115. Hell. 5.4.1.
116. 7.5.12.
117. 5.2.18.
118. 6.1.2-3. He would later be executed by Polyphron, successor tyrant to Jason: 6.4.34.
119. 7.2.1ff.
120. 6.5.38.
121. 6.5.43.
122. 6.5.41. Note his use of the phrase εἰς τὸν ἅπαντα χρόνον (for all time), which is a catch-phrase in numerous inscriptions of the period. The frequency of its repetition gives the lie to the very alliances which so proclaimed their own eternity.
123. 7.1.2-3, 7.1.5-6, 7.1.9.
124. 7.1.11.
125. The next speaker, the Athenian Kephisodotos, also points out other weaknesses in Prokles' plan, although his own advice, subsequently accepted, is not necessarily the best either.
126. Cf. Hans Breitenbach, "Xenophon," article in Pauly-Wissowa, Realencyclopädie der Altertumswissenschaft, Vol. 18, second series, col. 1647.
127. Hell. 6.5.35.
128. 6.3.6.
129. Cf. Sordi, "I caratteri dell'opera storiographica . . ." Part 2, p. 346; also Elisabeth Vorrenhagen, De orationibus quae sunt in Xenophontis Hellenicis (Elberfeld, 1926), p. 105. Cf., e.g., Isokrates 4. 54-5.
130. Hell. 6.3.10.
131. 6.3.16.
132. 6.3.11.
133. 2.4.42.
134. 2.4.40.
135. For a different view, cf. H.D. Westlake, "Individuals in Xenophon,

'Hellenica,'" *Bulletin of the John Rylands Library* 49 (1966): 246ff., now in *Essays on the Greek Historians and Greek History* (Manchester, 1969), pp. 203ff. He tries to argue that Xenophon could only appreciate the mediocre and popular leader and not, like Thucydides, the great man capable of making a great impact on history. But even he cannot get around Xenophon's presentation of Epameinondas (about which he errs, by the way, in saying that Xenophon nowhere understands the enlightened statesmanship of the Theban leader—cf. 7.1.42-3, 7.4.10ff.); and he does not adequately comprehend the complexity of Xenophon's presentation of Lysander, because he has not first examined how and why Xenophon has structured his narrative as he has. Although he has modified his views somewhat, the attitude and approach remain the same in his more recent "Xenophon and Epameinondas," *Greek, Roman, and Byzantine Studies* 16 (1975): 23ff. It should also be pointed out that, if there is no one as singled out in the *Hellenika* for intellectual rigor as various figures in Thucydides are, the reason may not lie in Xenophon's small-mindedness but in the fact that there were no Themistokles and Perikles to write about. That Xenophon did have some regard for Themistokles and Perikles can be seen at *Mem.* 2.6.13, 3.6.2, 4.2.2. On similar concerns in Thucydides and Xenophon, cf. the remarks of Virginia Hunter, *Thucydides, The Artful Reporter* (Toronto, 1973) on *pleonexia*, pp. 79ff., and her statement, p. 180, " 'Ταραχή' seems in fact to have haunted the historian." E. M. Soulis's sorry book *Xenophon and Thucydides* (Athens, 1972) does nothing to further the study of the connection between the two authors. The seemingly personal bias against Xenophon displayed on p. 189 ("the 'hippie' of the fourth century") hardly moves beyond the nationalist Niebuhr's strictures, and the whole methodology of the study is either misconceived or misapplied. Parallels cited in the texts of the two historians are often mere commonplaces which could be paralleled elsewhere, unjust criticisms of Xenophon's inclusion of details are frequently made (cf., e.g., the example on p. 34 where the allegedly insignificant weather report explains how Alkibiades saw what he did), and all sorts of unfounded aprioristic reasoning used to impugn the accuracy of Xenophon's reports (cf., e.g., the simple denial of Hermokrates' being able to lament his unjust cashiering and advising his soldiers to remain loyal to the home authorities: and yet, as a citation on p. 185 shows, Soulis has read the *Kriton!*). The sheer idiocy of many remarks like "I do not think Xenophon capable of writing a historical novel" (p. 33)—what about the *Kyroupaideia?*—beggars charity.

136. Xenophon's lapses must surely be due to his haste more than to his poor judgment, if lapses they be. For if the unitarian view be accepted, the *Hellenika* was conceived and written in a much briefer time than Thucydides' history. Even so Xenophon is not unaware of conflicting versions of an event and of the problem of choosing between them: cf. 3.5.17-25 or 5.4.7. He was, at least, an honest reporter of what he knew. As for his omissions, they cannot be dismissed simply as the result of bias

or insufficient research. Omissions in the first two books may be explained by the fact that Xenophon did not mean to provide a fully detailed account of the purely military aspects of the conclusion of the Peloponnesian War; as the length of the excurses on the trial of the generals and on the Thirty shows, he was more interested in other things. As for the notorious failure to mention the foundation of the Second Athenian Confederacy and the establishment of an independent Messene, it should be realized, first of all, that Xenophon does not conceal the effect of these occurrences. Secondly, owing to the structure of his account, the narrative might have been derailed if these events were recorded at the chronologically appropriate time. When Xenophon could have spoken about the Confederacy, he has centered his account around internal affairs in Sparta and not in Athens. It may also be that modern scholars in their passion for facts are more enamoured of the Aristoteles Decree than contemporaries were. A direct parallel comes to mind in Thucydides' failure to mention the increase in the tribute in 425/4. The view that Thucydides would have included a mention if he had lived to finish his history is mere guesswork. This might be especially so if the *Hellenika* was written in the period 361-355, when the Confederacy had long been minus the Thebans and was in process of losing other allies in the Social War. To contemporaries the Decree may have been of only archival interest at most. Likewise, concerning Messene, no contemporary was likely to have been unaware of what happened here and of Epameinondas' role, so Xenophon may have felt no necessity to spell it out. Finally it is certainly doubtful that Xenophon's inaccuracies of detail, whatever they may be, discredit in any significant way his interpretation of the course of events.

137. *Hell.* 2.3.56.
138. 5.1.4.
139. 4.8.18-9, 6.2.19, 5.4.25ff., 4.8.38, 3.1.21ff.
140. 4.8.25ff., esp. 4.8.30-1. Is it for this reason that Xenophon says in Thrasyboulos' obituary that he "seemed" to be a good man rather than he "was" one?
141. Or the Spartans could resist all good and proper sense and diplomacy; for Leuktra occurred soon after the successful realization of Kallistratos' proposals.
142. Cf. *Mem.* 4.2.40.
143. *How to write history* 39.

Chapter 7

1. Diogenes Laertios 2.56, 2.58.
2. 2.53, 2.59. It is customarily agreed that the date of Xenophon's recall must have occurred soon after the rapprochement between Athens and Sparta which developed in 371/70. An earlier recall is unlikely because

even in the periods of peace, as, for example, after 387, there was hardly what could be called goodwill between the two cities.

3. *Hell.* 7.5.16.

4. 7.4.4-5.

5. On this development, cf. the magisterial work of Gustave Glotz, *La solidarité de la famille* (Paris, 1904), pp. 413ff.

6. *Ibid.*, p. 415.

7. On this point, cf. W.K. Lacey, *The Family in Classical Greece* (London, 1968), p. 218.

8. *Ibid.*, pp. 75-76.

9. *Ekklesiazousai* 221ff.

10. *Ibid.*, 304ff. (Ussher).

11. Cf., e.g., *Olynthiac* 3.21ff.

12. For a general survey, cf. the essay by J. Dörig, "The Late Classical Period," in *Greek Art and Architecture* (Abrams, New York, no date), pp. 433ff., who can state that "the relationship of Late Classical to Classical art is that of dream to reality."

13. Thuc. 2.36.

14. ll. 577ff.

15. *Mem.*, 4.4.6.

16. *Mem.*, 2.1.

17. *Mem.*, 4.1.1.

18. "Quellenuntersuchungen zur griechischen Geschichte," *Rheinisches Museum* 44 (1889), p. 192. Also in *Gesammelte Schriften* (Berlin, 1956), Vol. 2, p. 172. Schwartz's argument of course does not *prove* composition within a narrow space of time, but that view is strengthened by the realization that in speaking of cross-references and repetitions he is referring to more than common ideas and turns of phrase which any author might use frequently over a quite long writing career, but to extensive and almost verbatim repetitions, e.g., those in the *Hell.* and *Ages.*, the *Apol.* and *Mem.*

19. Agesilaos died in 360.

20. For the date, cf. Gabriella Bodei Giglioni's edition of the *Poroi* (Florence, 1970), pp. vii-viii.

21. See Chapter Seven, notes 27 and 58.

22. See Chapter Four, note 10.

23. See Chapter Three, note 22.

24. The *Oik.* may be contemporary with the *Hi.* if the view of Strauss is accepted that the two works are contrasting complements, one dealing with tyranny, the other with proper civic life. The conversation between the younger Perikles and Socrates in *Mem.* 3.5 suggests a date after 370, since it is so concerned in the topics discussed with border defense against the Boiotians. Also it seems unlikely that Xenophon could have written the dialogue with Aristippos concerning the futility of life as a stranger at 2.1, if he still remained unharassed at Skillous. If the interpretation of the *CofL* given in chapter four is correct, a date after Xenophon's

return to Athens for the composition of this work is more likely.

25. Strauss, by contrast, tends to stress the earlier, free-wheeling activities of Xenophon as forming the decisive influence on his intellectual outlook. Cf. *On Tyranny* (London, 1963), pp. 101-2.

26. *Menexenos* 235d1ff.

27. This serious concern was probably motivated by the ascendancy of Thebes after 371. Cf. esp. 7.2-3. A date in the Sixties is therefore reasonable.

28. *Hipp.* 1.8.

29. 6.4ff., 1.5ff.

30. 1.8.

31. 3.1ff.

32. 3.13. Note also at 5.10 Xenophon's unsentimental advice to observe the deception practiced by children in their game of "how much?"

33. 5.9.

34. 5.11.

35. *Ibid.*

36. 8.7-8.

37. 4.13.

38. 8.1-2.

39. 4.5, 8.16, 8.21.

40. *Mem.* 3.3.

41. It is to be noted that, save for a passing mention in *Mem.* 4.4.1., Xenophon is silent about Socrates as a soldier. Cf. Olaf Gigon, *Kommentar zum ersten Buch von Xenophons Memorabilien* (Basel, 1953), p. 26, and Leo Strauss, *Xenophon's Socratic Discourse* (Ithaca, 1970), p. 88.

42. *Oik.* 11.4.

43. *P.H.* 2.1ff.

44. For the frequent comparison of horses and humans in Xenophon, cf., e.g., *Hi.* 10.2, *Oik.* 3.10, *Sym.* 2.10, *Mem.* 4.1.3, *Kyro.* 7.5.62.

45. *P.H.* 11.6.

46. 9.2, 6.13.

47. Cf. 1.7, 1.14, 3.6.

48. 9.7, 7.1, 8.1.

49. 4.1.

50. 12.14.

51. 1.1.

52. *Ibid.* A floruit of 424 for Simon is suggested by Pollux 2.69 who records a criticism of the mid-fifth century artist Mikon made by Simon and by the mention of a hipparch Simon at Aristophanes *Knights* 242. His awkward prose also suggests a fifth-century date. For a discussion of the similarities and differences between Simon and Xenophon, cf. J. Soukup, "De libello Simonis Atheniensis de re equestri," in *Commentationes Aenipontanae* 6 (1911) and the edition of the *P.H.* by E. Delebecque (Paris, 1950), pp. 155ff.

53. *Mem.* 1.7.1. Cf. also Cyrus' perception at *Kyro.* 8.1.37.

54. *P.H.* 11.8-9, 13. Cf. Delebecque, ed. of the *P.H.*, pp. 24-5.
55. *P.H.* 11.3.
56. 12.1ff.
57. 11.10. Cf. *Hipp.* 1.22.
58. *P.H.* 12.14. The last chapter is clearly integral to the whole (Xenophon has mentioned danger earlier in the treatise), and Delebecque's attempt, ed. of the *P.H.*, pp. 17-8, to make it a later addition and thus to secure a date much earlier than the *Hipp.* for the composition of the rest of the *P.H.* is contrived and unconvincing. The *P.H.* is to be dated in the mid-sixties or later.
59. 2.1. Cf. also *Hipp* 1.12 where the good calvary commander is said to put an end to youthful extravagance while making youths good riders.
60. *Mem.* 3.1.5ff. Also cf. *Kyro.* 1.6.12ff.
61. *Por.* 1.2ff.
62. 2.1ff. and 3.1ff. On metics in the cavalry (2.5), cf. the earlier suggestion in *Hipp.* 9.6. It should be noted, however, how Xenophon insists on removing foreigners from the army proper: *Por.* 2.3.
63. *Por.* 4.1ff.
64. 4.32.
65. It is refreshing to see at last a careful distinction made between the views of Xenophon and Isokrates, such as Giglioni has done now, ed. of the *Por.*, pp. xxiii-xxiv, xxvi, xxviii.
66. *Por.* 5.8.
67. 5.13.
68. The statement of that inveterate admirer of Euboulos, G.L. Cawkwell, goes too far in maintaining that the *Por.* proposes what Euboulos enacted ("Eubulus," *Journal of Hellenic Studies* 83 [1963]: 56). To say the least, it is hard to imagine Xenophon agreeing with the plump kind of society Euboulos sought to preserve at all costs—note Xenophon's rejection of a mercenary army—or that he who had so admired the initiative of Agesilaos and Iphikrates in taking the war to the enemy's own territory would have applauded the sluggishness of Euboulos' policy against Philip. Needless to say the fact that Euboulos may have been responsible for securing Xenophon's recall from exile does not imply anything about their political friendship. It can simply be seen as the act of an up-and-coming politician trying to gain some publicity by sponsoring a measure involving a prominent person.
69. *Por.* 1.1.
70. *Sym.* 4.1.
71. Contrast, e.g., *Mem.* 4.2.9 with the assertions in *Hi.* 9.7-10.
72. *Por.* 6.1.
73. *Sym.* 2.11, *Mem.* 1.3.9.
74. Plutarch, *Sulla* 6.2.
75. *Mem.* 1.1.9.
76. Cf., e.g., Antiphanes, frgm. 33, and Amphis, frgm. 13 (Edmonds), and Plutarch, *De adulatore et amico* 9 and *De audiendis poetis* 8.

77. *Anab.* 3.2.11ff., when Xenophon is trying to raise despairing spirits after the loss of the generals.
78. Cf., e.g., *Por.* 5.5-7, *Kyro.* (!) 8.7.24.
79. *P.H.* 11.13.
80. *Sym.* 8.43.
81. *Hipp.* 1.1 and *passim*; 9.8.
82. 9.1.
83. *Mem.* 1.1.7.
84. *Por.* 6.2-3.

INDEX

Agesilaos, 4, 5, 22, 23, 48, 76ff., 104ff., 111, 112, 116, 121, 168, 171, 176, 178.
Agesilaos, 76ff., 85, 96, 101, 106, 131, 132, 137, 151, 168, 176.
alazōn, 6, 13, 16, 39, 41, 47, 49, 53, 72, 78, 80.
Alkibiades, 24, 36, 37, 111, 113, 171, 174.
Anabasis, 2, 7, 10, 23, 82ff., 101, 132.
analogy, 25, 40.
anger (and passion in general), 11, 33, 39, 81, 85, 112, 113, 124, 133, 135, 171, 172.
animals, 26, 45, 46, 79, 90, 116. See also "horses."
Antisthenes, 16, 17, 20, 44, 147, 148, 160.
Apology, 12, 25, 40ff., 176.
Arginousai, 12, 104, 111, 113, 119.
Aristippos, 25, 26, 31, 36, 64, 131, 151, 176.
Aristophanes, 130, 135, 137, 148, 177.
Aristotle, 1, 13, 26, 148, 151, 152, 154, 157, 158, 162.
Artaxerxes, 23, 84, 85, 86.
Athens, 11, 22, 24, 40, 66, 67, 73, 82, 89, 92, 96, 98, 99, 104, 106, 107, 111, 113, 114, 115, 117, 118, 121, 122, 125, 126, 128ff., 150, 164.
Augustine, 73, 155.
Austen, Jane, 145.
autarkeia, 36, 138, 139, 142, 153, 154.

Autokles, 107, 122.
autonomy, See "freedom."

chance (and uncertainty), 19, 33, 34, 39, 40, 79, 81, 84, 92, 95, 98, 103, 104, 110, 114, 119, 123, 124, 134, 138, 140, 142, 159.
city, See "*polis*."
confusion, 33, 51, 85, 87, 90, 108, 110, 113, 117, 123, 127, 130, 138, 174.
Constitution of the Lacedaemonians, 65ff., 132.
cosmopolitanism, 4, 44, 127, 141.
Croesus, 48, 52, 53, 54.
Cyrus the Great, 44ff., 60, 63, 64, 66, 163, 177.
Cyrus the Younger, 11, 22, 23, 24, 82ff., 94, 95, 96, 98, 128, 132, 140.

deceit, 56, 63, 70, 81, 82, 83, 84, 86, 87, 93, 96, 98, 104, 105, 108, 109, 118, 133, 134, 177.
Delphi, 22, 42, 69, 82, 96, 123, 142.
Diodoros the Sicilian, 93, 94.
Diogenes Laertios, 22, 23, 128, 147, 160, 167, 169.
Dostoevsky, 145.

economy, 7, 9, 18, 35, 38, 72, 136, 138ff.
envy, 33, 42, 75, 155.
Epameinondas, 48, 116ff., 126, 127, 141, 174, 175.
Ephoros, 93, 94, 165.

180

INDEX 181

Euphron, 109, 110, 115, 118, 121.

family, 19, 27, 28, 44, 45, 55, 57, 61, 64, 66, 68, 71, 73, 77, 78, 81, 85, 88, 89, 90, 97, 114, 129, 157.
farming, 29, 32, 33, 34, 46, 66, 97, 132, 152, 153, 154.
fatherland, See "*polis.*"
force, 38, 39, 40, 45, 49, 50, 61, 68, 69, 75, 107, 108, 126, 134, 135, 138.
freedom, 37, 39, 45, 46, 50, 51, 53, 67, 68, 70, 71, 72, 80, 81, 86, 88, 103ff., 109, 111, 128, 129, 135.
friends, 16, 19, 26, 27, 28, 34ff., 40, 45, 48, 52, 55, 61, 64, 71, 72, 73, 76, 78, 82, 83, 112, 117, 121, 129, 135, 136, 161.

Gibbon, 1, 166.
glory, See "*philotimia.*"
gods, 10, 17, 19, 26, 29ff., 39, 41, 45, 54, 56, 58, 62, 64, 78, 87, 96, 97, 98, 114, 119, 120, 121, 133, 136, 140, 142, 152. See also "Delphi."
gratitude, See "indebtedness."
Grote, George, 23, 99.

Hellenika, 5, 9, 67, 76, 96, 99ff., 128, 129, 132, 134, 138, 140, 176.
Herodotos, 4, 44, 157, 166.
Hiero, 60ff., 73, 131, 176.
Hipparkhikos, 131, 133ff., 142.
Homer, 16, 18, 54, 89, 96, 146, 149, 166.
honor, See "*philotimia.*"
horses, 35, 51, 85, 135ff., 153, 177.
humor (and play), 9, 12ff., 18, 20, 35, 41, 49, 50, 56, 60, 62, 63, 65, 72, 85, 87, 109, 115, 133, 156, 159, 161.
hunting, 46, 47, 50, 69, 97, 132.

idiōtēs, See "individual (and individuation)."

increase, 27, 29, 33, 35, 47, 77, 106, 108, 123, 154. See also "*pleonexia*" and "wealth."
indebtedness, 27, 45, 71, 74, 76, 80, 128, 129, 139, 151.
individual (and individuation), 4, 21, 22, 25, 26, 30, 31, 51, 52, 54, 56, 57, 61, 62, 63, 67, 69, 71, 73, 74, 75, 77, 83, 90, 106, 108, 117, 120, 122, 125, 128ff., 134, 136, 137, 140, 141, 142, 154, 155.
Iphikrates, 112, 121, 141, 178.
irony, 13, 14, 15, 20, 56, 72, 87, 104, 155.
Iskhomakhos, 28ff., 33, 34, 35, 37, 62, 65, 153.
Isokrates, 8, 11, 48, 72, 94, 97, 98, 122, 129, 130, 138, 167, 173, 178.

Jason of Pherai, 60, 103, 104, 110, 115, 118, 120, 160, 171, 173.
justice, 24, 26, 28, 30ff., 37, 38, 41, 45, 46, 47, 57, 66, 70, 79, 82, 92, 105, 107, 115, 123, 127, 139.

Kallias, 3, 9, 15ff., 35, 122, 138, 142, 149.
Kallikratidas, 10ff., 105, 111, 112, 172.
Kallistratos of Aphidna, 122, 123, 127, 175.
Kharmides, 3, 17, 31, 159.
Kinadon, 115ff.
Klearkhos, 10, 84ff., 165.
Knidos, 104, 111, 112.
Konon, 11, 111, 172.
Koroneia, 77, 79, 168.
Kounaxa, 85, 86, 95, 145.
Kritias, 24, 37, 75, 108, 109, 171.
Kritoboulos, 3, 15, 18, 19, 27, 28, 29, 33ff., 140, 148.
Ktesias, 44, 94, 95, 165.
Kyroupaideia, 6, 44ff., 66, 101, 125, 132, 174.

labor, 19, 25, 26, 37, 50, 51, 52, 78, 80, 89, 92, 117, 133, 134, 138, 157.

law, See "nomos."
Leuktra, 48, 110, 117, 118, 119, 121, 162, 168, 172, 173, 175.
limit, 27ff., 38, 40, 42, 47, 52, 77, 79, 126.
love, 15ff., 21, 26, 38, 53, 56, 62, 77, 112, 113, 140, 147, 148, 149, 154, 172.
Lykourgos, 66ff.
Lysander, 10ff., 22, 102, 104, 105, 107, 111, 112, 170, 174.

Machiavelli, 1, 35, 155, 158.
Mantineia, 104, 107, 117, 118, 120, 128, 168.
Marx, 157.
Memorabilia, 25ff., 131, 137, 140, 142, 176.
money, See "wealth."
mutability, 1, 59, 111ff., 115, 120, 141. See also "chance (and uncertainty)."

Niebuhr, B.G., 1, 99, 100, 123, 174.
nomos, 24, 28, 29, 30ff., 39, 55, 57, 60, 65, 66, 69, 70, 75, 82, 96, 107, 114, 116, 123, 126.

Oikonomikos, 25, 28ff., 32, 34, 38, 176.
order, 7, 13, 14, 21, 29, 30, 32, 33, 34, 45, 50, 51, 88, 104, 117, 123, 135, 137.

panhellenism, 11, 97, 129.
Pantheia, 6, 53.
passion, See "anger."
Pausanias, 108, 111, 113, 168, 172.
Peri Hippikēs, 131, 135ff.
Persia, 10, 33, 44, 48, 66, 77, 79ff., 97, 106, 110, 111, 112, 117, 119, 122, 130, 158, 161.
persuasion, 38, 45, 135.
philotimia, 26, 28, 34, 36, 37, 46, 55, 56, 58, 73, 76, 79, 81, 83, 88, 91, 96, 97, 98, 111, 113, 117, 118, 124, 126, 130, 132, 136, 139, 140, 171, 172.
Phoibidas, 107, 112.
Plato, 1, 21, 24, 39, 58, 60, 102, 141, 152, 154, 155, 162, 174, 177.
pleonexia, 28, 30, 36, 38, 46, 47, 63, 64, 67, 77, 78, 104, 107, 108, 115, 117, 123, 126, 128, 133, 138, 172, 174.
Plutarch, 93, 145, 165, 172, 178.
polis (and fatherland*), 18, 19, 24, 26, 29ff., 36, 38, 45*, 56, 60, 64, 67, 70, 71, 77*, 79*, 82*, 88*, 89, 90, 91, 96, 108, 117*, 120, 125, 127, 128ff., 134, 135, 137, 138, 142, 154, 155*.
Poroi, 126, 131, 138ff., 142.
power, See "*pleonexia*."
professionalism, 129, 134, 137, 140.
Prokles, 121, 122, 123, 173.
Proxenos, 82, 84, 86, 87, 93.

risk, See "chance (and uncertainty)."
Rousseau, 128.

self-satisfaction, 16, 17, 18, 38, 71.
self-sufficiency, See "*autarkeia*."
Skillous, 23, 76, 94, 96, 98, 128, 132, 153, 161, 167, 176.
slavery, 25, 26, 37, 48, 79, 86, 106.
Socrates, 1, 2, 3, 8, 12ff., 21ff., 54, 55, 56, 64, 66, 82, 92, 98, 123, 127, 130, 131, 132, 134, 136, 137, 139ff., 146ff., 153, 154, 177.
Sophainetos, 93, 94, 167.
sophists, 15, 19, 24, 26, 30, 36, 37, 38, 40, 66, 83, 129, 130, 132, 151.
Sparta, 6, 9, 11, 17, 23, 24, 48, 65ff., 77ff., 89, 104, 105, 107, 110, 111, 115ff., 121, 122, 126, 148, 161, 164, 173.
specificity, 2, 4, 5, 7, 8, 13, 50, 56, 97, 137.
speech, 9, 10, 32, 40, 41, 84, 87, 88,

104, 106, 124, 155, 161. See also "words."
Sphodrias, 107, 112, 115, 124.
style, 2ff., 54, 60, 61, 62, 65, 66, 69, 72, 75, 76, 94, 101, 109, 124, 133, 136, 141, 154.
Symposium, 3, 15ff., 35, 139, 140, 142, 159.

Taine, H., 7, 8.
tarakhē, See "confusion."
Teleutias, 112, 113, 124.
Ten Thousand, the, 6, 10, 22, 23, 94, 97.
Thebes (Boiotia), 9, 104, 106, 107, 110, 111, 116, 118, 121, 162, 176, 177.
Themistogenes of Syracuse, 93, 98.
Theramenes, 12, 13, 108, 109, 114, 124.
Thrasyboulos, 116, 122, 126, 127, 172, 175.
Thucydides, 4, 8, 99ff., 104, 123ff., 127, 169, 174, 175.
Timotheos, 140, 172.
Tissaphernes, 10, 87, 88, 91, 115.
Tocqueville, A. de, 109.
travel, 22, 46, 79, 81, 82, 84, 88, 95, 96, 98, 129, 130, 132, 142, 166.
tyranny, 17, 19, 40, 46, 60ff., 67, 72, 73, 75, 103, 105, 107, 108, 114, 125, 129, 157.
Tyrants, Thirty, 17, 24, 63, 75, 100, 103, 106, 113, 116, 150, 152, 175. See also "Kharmides," "Kritias," and "Theramenes."

uncertainty, See "chance (and uncertainty)."

war (and enemies), 28, 32, 33, 40, 41, 47, 50, 51, 52, 61, 65, 70, 71, 73, 77, 81, 84, 103, 105, 124, 133, 134, 138, 171, 177.
wealth, 16, 17, 18, 34ff., 45, 67, 68, 78, 79, 83, 86, 88, 90, 92, 108, 109, 111, 123, 124, 129, 138, 154, 155.
wonder, 1, 42, 53, 55, 58, 72, 73, 92.
words, 3, 4, 7, 12, 13, 41, 43, 52, 56, 60, 105, 141. See also "speech."

Xenophon, birth, 149; death, 128; exile, 22ff., 76, 96, 98, 99, 128, 133, 143, 150, 162; laconism, 22, 23, 66, 99, 119.

www.ingramcontent.com/pod-product-compliance
Lightning Source LLC
Chambersburg PA
CBHW021758230426
43669CB00006B/120